SONIA JOHNSON

Introductions to Mormon Thought

Edited by Matthew Bowman and Joseph M. Spencer
*For a list of books in the series, please see our website
at* www.press.uillinois.edu.

SONIA JOHNSON

A Mormon Feminist

CHRISTINE TALBOT

**UNIVERSITY OF
ILLINOIS PRESS**
Urbana, Chicago, and Springfield

Library of Congress Cataloging-in-Publication Data

Names: Talbot, Christine, author.
Title: Sonia Johnson : a Mormon feminist / Christine
Talbot. Other titles: Introductions to Mormon
thought.
Description: Urbana : University of Illinois Press,
[2024] | Series: Introductions to Mormon thought |
Includes bibliographical references and index.
Identifiers: LCCN 2024000391 (print) | LCCN
2024000392 (ebook) | ISBN 9780252046063
(cloth) | ISBN 9780252088179 (paperback) | ISBN
9780252047244 (ebook)
Subjects: LCSH: Johnson, Sonia. | Latter Day Saint
women—United States—Biography. | Feminists—
United States—Biography. | Feminism—Religious
aspects—Church of Jesus Christ of Latter-day Saints.
| LCGFT: Biographies.
Classification: LCC BX8695.J65 T35 2024 (print)
|LCC BX8695.J65 (ebook) | DDC 289.3092 [B]—dc23/
eng/20240331
LC record available at https://lccn.loc.gov/2024000391
LC ebook record available at https://lccn.loc.
gov/2024000392

Contents

Foreword to the
Introductions to Mormon Thought Series   vii
  Matthew Bowman and Joseph M. Spencer

Acknowledgments   ix

CHAPTER ONE
"Patriarchy Is a Sham": A Short Biography of Sonia Johnson   1

CHAPTER TWO
"Well, I'm About to Find Out":
Disciplining Mormons, Disciplining Feminism   22

CHAPTER THREE
"A Compromise with Integrity that It Simply Cannot Afford":
The Gendered Ethics of Revelation, Religion, and Politics   47

CHAPTER FOUR
"The Grossest Misuses of Women's Religious Convictions":
Gender, Honesty, and Accountability   65

Bibliographic Essay   85

Notes   97

Index   117

Foreword to the Introductions
to Mormon Thought Series

Our purpose in this series is to provide readers with accessible and short
introductions to important figures in the intellectual life of the religious
movement that traces its origins to the prophetic career of Joseph Smith
Jr. With an eye to the many branches of that movement (rather than solely
to its largest branch, the Church of Jesus Christ of Latter-day Saints), the
series gathers studies of what scholars have long called *Mormon* thought.
We define "thought" and "intellectual life," however, quite as broadly as we
define "Mormonism." We understand these terms to be inclusive, not simply of formal theological or scholarly work but also of artistic production,
devotional writing, institutional influence, political activism, and other
nonscholarly pursuits. In short, volumes in the series assess the contributions of men and women who have shaped how those called Mormons in
various traditions think about what "Mormonism" is.

We hope that this series marks something of a coming of age of scholarship on this religious tradition. For many years, Mormon studies has
focused primarily on historical questions largely of internal interest to
the (specifically) Latter-day Saints community. Such historical work has
also mainly addressed the nineteenth century. Scholars have accordingly
established the key sources for the study of Mormon history and culture,
and they have established a broad consensus on many issues surrounding
the origins and character of the religious movement. Recent work, however,
has pushed academics into the work of comparison, asking larger questions
in two key ways. First, recent scholars have approached these topics from
a greater variety of disciplines. There has emerged in Mormon studies, in
other words, increasing visibility for the disciplines of philosophy, sociology,

literary criticism, and media studies, among others. Second, scholars working this field have also begun to consider new topics of study—in particular, gender and sexuality, the status of international Mormonism, and the experience of minority groups within the tradition. We believe the field has thus reached the point where the sort of syntheses these books offer is both possible and needed.

Christine Talbot's study of Sonia Johnson is an ideal contribution to the field. Because of her own background and training, Talbot brings Sonia into conversation not simply with the religious tradition into which she was born and gained influence and fame, but also with the broader currents of second-wave American feminism. Talbot therefore successfully contextualizes Sonia's life and thought in two worlds at once. In so doing, she shows the benefits of comparison and contextualization. For Sonia, Mormonism and second-wave feminism informed each other. Further, though, Sonia's story shows for Talbot how scholarship informed by both religious studies and gender studies can deepen understanding of both fields. We are pleased to include her volume in *Introductions to Mormon Thought*.

Matthew Bowman
Joseph M. Spencer

Foreword to the Introductions to Mormon Thought Series

Acknowledgments

I owe the completion of this project to many people. Several archivists at the LDS Church History Library of the Church of Jesus Christ of Latter-day Saints helped find and make accessible several necessary sources, most especially Anne Berryhill and Sarah Palmer but also Ashley Holdaway, Elise Reynolds, and Audrey Spainhower. Elizabeth Rogers and Molly Rose Steed at the J. Willard Marriot Library, University of Utah Special Collections department were also especially helpful, as was Clint Pumphrey at the Merrill-Cazier Library, Special Collections and Archives Division at Utah State University. University of Northern Colorado librarians Wendy Highby and Jennifer Leffler helped me find sometimes obscure references, while graduate students Roger Wadsworth and Ezra Taylor helped with library legwork and transcriptions of audiovisual material. Series editors Matthew Bowman and Joseph Spencer and my editor Alison Syring at the University of Illinois Press provided most needed feedback that significantly strengthened the manuscript. My thanks as well to friends and colleagues who read and commented on portions of this manuscript, including Wendy Highby, Kyle Nelson, Linda Curtis, Mees Tielens, Taylor Petrey, Jennifer Wojciechowski, Amanda Hendrix-Komoto, and the anonymous reader for the University of Illinois Press. I also acknowledge support from the University of Northern Colorado Faculty Research and Publications Board (FRPB). Finally, my deepest gratitude goes to those who helped but would rather their names not be associated with the project. They know who they are.

CHAPTER ONE

"Patriarchy Is a Sham"
A Short Biography of Sonia Johnson

Few people in the history of the Mormon faith community provoke such varied and visceral responses as Sonia Johnson. Few issues in Mormon history have been as contentious or as well publicized as Sonia's excommunication from the Church of Jesus Christ of Latter-day Saints (LDS or Mormon church).[1] Sonia's excommunication tapped into deep-seated tensions within the Mormon community about gender, equality, power, and authority. Between 1977 and 1982, the years before and after her December 1979 excommunication, Sonia experienced a heartbreaking but enlightening feminist awakening, founded a political organization, endured a very public and painful excommunication from the LDS church through which she became a national media sensation, underwent a difficult and public divorce, became a well-known and controversial feminist speaker and activist, and served as the most visible public face of LDS feminism to the world outside of the church. Over those years, she traveled far from her former life as a fairly traditional Mormon housewife (though one with a doctoral degree who taught college classes) to become one of the church's most renowned, most loved, most reviled, and perhaps most misunderstood dissidents. Nearly all of her public activities, especially those regarding her excommunication, were well covered in the national press.

The Equal Rights Amendment (ERA) was the arena within which Sonia's battle against the church was fought, but the contests were about gender, power, agency, and authority. The sides of the debate took shape quickly, if not always clearly: Sonia and her supporters on one side, the church and its representatives on the other, and many people, LDS and non-LDS, somewhere in between. Sonia's experience confronting the church and the church's response to her criticisms are conduits through which this book explores critical cultural, political, and religious questions about LDS thought, culture, and belief emerging from her ideas and her situation. Sonia's experience with and interpretations and critiques of the church served as a flashpoint for Mormonism's confrontation with mainstream feminism in the late 1970s and early 1980s.

Sonia's support of the ERA and critiques of church patriarchy, especially as they played out on a national stage, shaped the landscape on which contemporary feminist Mormons navigate the difficult territory between faith and feminism. In her years as the most publicly visible face of Mormon feminism, Sonia publicly articulated a profound spiritual and political anguish many LDS women have felt under church patriarchy, especially in the wake of and since the church's opposition to the ERA. Before and after her excommunication, Sonia aired the church's dirty laundry in public. She exposed the political strategies male church leaders and (mostly women) members used to defeat the ERA. Her critiques of the church and its leaders resonated with hundreds if not thousands of church members, men and women. Sonia also provoked the church itself—both its leaders and its members—to confront critical issues of gender, power, agency, and authority in the wake of the women's movement.

Most of what we know about Sonia's excommunication and the years prior to it comes from Sonia herself. Understandably, the church does not comment on excommunication procedures, and until a few weeks after Sonia's excommunication, it was also fairly quiet in the press about its opposition to the ERA. Reporters had a difficult time finding church representatives to speak with.[2] Sonia's archival collections contain hundreds of newspaper articles and several hours of recordings of her speaking publicly about her experiences and about church politics in radio and television interviews, at political rallies and events, and at universities and organizations. Recordings of her speaking privately with friends or just into a tape recorder also remain. These, plus a large collection of newspaper articles and other documents central to her excommunication and subsequent activism, along with thousands of letters, both sympathetic to and critical of Sonia, are in her collections at the Special Collections Department of the J. Willard Marriott Library at the University of Utah in Salt Lake City.

Although Sonia discussed many of her life events in her 1981 memoir, *From Housewife to Heretic*, memoirs by their very nature are written with the advantages of hindsight. By necessity, they also construct a coherent narrative out of events usually lived much more chaotically in the moment. For this reason, this account relies, when possible, on more immediate sources created closer to the time they occurred and with less curation, reflection, and revision. I also privilege those sources that reached the widest audiences and had the biggest effect and have relied more on Sonia's speeches and interviews over press coverage containing a reporter's gloss. (This is also because Sonia was frequently misquoted in the press.) I have also relied primarily on public appearances and interviews of church representatives for the same reasons. I have made minor grammatical changes and deletions to account for the vagaries of the spoken word so that utterances appear in complete grammatically correct sentences.

Sonia's Early Feminist Stirrings

Sonia Ann Harris Johnson was born in Malad, Idaho in 1936 to Alvin Harris and Ida Lavina Howell Harris. She lived in Preston, Idaho until she was twelve, when the family moved to Logan, Utah and was baptized a member of the Church of Jesus Christ of Latter-day Saints in March 1944. In accounts from the 1980s, Sonia reports her childhood fairly positively, including lots of wonderful times in nature. However, the third of five children, Sonia felt she grew up in a family without much warmth, raised by parents who "were not happy together."[3] Early feminist stirrings emerged as Sonia watched her brothers exempted from chores required of her and her sister and saw her father treat her mother badly. Watching doors open to her brothers but close to her because she was born a female made her "progressively less happy as my childhood went on."[4] Sonia now asserts an even less idyllic picture, disclosing that her father emotionally abused her mother and that her eldest brother, whom Sonia believed her parents favored, abused her badly for much of her childhood.[5]

Sonia deeply respected her mother, who was "born with superior intelligence and extraordinary gifts as an organizer, an administrator, a financier, and an artist." She grew to resent how much family life had constrained her mother, turning her "into a timid, frustrated woman."[6] Sonia's mother had been raised in a very mystical LDS family in which nearly everyone had or knew someone who had experienced a miracle or seen spirits. When Sonia was growing up, her mother maintained a nearly constant conversation with

4

Jesus, praying nearly all the time. Johnson was much more attracted to her mother's more mystical, God- and Christ-centered practice of Mormonism than her father's vision, which she described as rooted in fear of a punitive God.[7]

Moments in Sonia's adolescence foreshadow her later feminism. When she was fifteen years old, a visiting instructor taught a Sunday school lesson on sexual modesty during which she plucked petals from a rose, each representing a vague act of physical intimacy, finally leaving only the stem of the rose. The instructor told the girls that, like the rose stem, they could never again be pure, so "no good man will ever want you."[8] The next week, the larger congregational meeting was fast and testimony meeting, an open meeting in which members bear testimony when they feel prompted. Sonia stood and told the congregation that the previous week's Sunday school message had been false doctrine that contradicted Jesus's teachings on repentance and forgiveness. Members of the ward, including the president of the Young Women organization, spent the rest of the meeting shaming Sonia for her words, and she was later chastened by both her best friend and her father. In a similar speech Sonia attended, then-apostle Mark E. Peterson likened girls allowing boys to kiss them to licking butter from a slice of bread. Sonia wondered, "What about the boys' butter?"[9] This event "completed my evolution into a lifelong foe of the double standard" that holds women more accountable for sexual behavior than men.[10] For the most part, though, Sonia kept these incidents compartmentalized from her more mystical faith and filed them away with little consideration.

Sonia graduated from Logan High School in 1954 and worked in a bank until January 1955, when she began attending Utah State University. She earned her bachelor's degree in English in 1958. About a year later, she married Richard (Rick) T. Johnson because, she recalled, he was the first boy to take her desires and needs seriously. As Sonia says in *From Housewife to Heretic*, unlike other boys she had dated, Rick "didn't live down to my expectations."[11] Both Rick and Sonia earned doctoral degrees, Sonia's with Rick's encouragement in education from Rutgers College. While in graduate school, Sonia gave birth to her first two children, Eric and Kari. Her third child, Marc, came along just after she got her first teaching job in Palo Alto, California. Sonia's first three pregnancies came with much nausea and the childbirths were difficult, long, and painful.

In Palo Alto, Sonia briefly associated with a group of LDS progressives, including Eugene England, who founded *Dialogue: A Journal of Mormon Thought* in 1966. She occasionally attended discussions England hosted at his home.[12] She made wonderful friends in the congregation there as well. During this time, the 1960s wave of church correlation increased the reach of patriarchal authority in the church. Intended to standardize church curriculum and instruction as the membership expanded, the process of correlation quickly expanded to bring auxiliary organizations under male control, including the church's children's organization called the Primary, the Young Women and Young Men organizations, and the Relief Society, the church's adult women's organization. As part of this effort, in 1967 the First Presidency of the church "recommend[ed] that only those who hold the priesthood be invited to offer the opening and closing prayers" in sacrament meetings.[13] Sonia found herself "thunderstruck" by and "aghast" about this policy shift that effectively removed from women the right to lead congregations in prayer. It felt arbitrarily punitive. Shortly after it was announced over the pulpit in every LDS congregation, Sonia experienced "a clear, crisp knowledge: this was *not* the way God behaved in his relationship with his children."[14] When she asked her bishop what women had done to incur such punishment, she did not get a satisfactory answer.[15] That policy was rescinded ten years later. In 1971, correlation processes stripped the Relief Society of its decision-making and financial autonomy and of its independent publication, *The Relief Society Magazine*.[16] Sonia later reflected that during this time, she "was learning that church leaders are not concerned about what harms women. They are concerned about how they can use women to build up the kingdom, build up male structure, not how the church can be useful to women."[17] The seeds of her feminist objections to church patriarchy were just beginning to take root.

Sonia was also raising three small children at this time and her relationship with motherhood was ambivalent. On the one hand, she loved her children, finding Eric "endlessly entrancing" and feeling "euphoric" that Kari was a girl, though she also "had difficulty regarding anything female as valuable." She said, "Until I discovered how much I admired and loved the woman in me, I did not admire it or love it properly in myself or anyone else, even my daughter. . . . I am indebted to the women's movement for truly giving me my daughter." She found Marc, her third child, the easiest and the most loving. At the same time, Sonia "chafed at the full-timeness" and sometimes boredom of motherhood, and Rick was "never very interested in parenting and consequently never did very much of it."[18] Her relationship with Rick was also sometimes quite troubled. Rick struggled with anxiety and worked a lot, and Sonia often found him emotionally closed and neglectful of her and the children. At times, this left her with only the children for company.

Sonia and Rick traveled quite a bit over the course of their twenty-year marriage and lived in several countries, including Samoa, Nigeria, Korea, and Malaysia, and several U.S. states as they followed Rick's education and career. This meant that they practiced their Mormonism mostly as a family away from the institutional church, a practice well suited to Sonia's more mystical faith. In feminist terms, Sonia's most transformative experiences were in Korea, where she had had two Korean housekeepers who took on the drudgery of housework, cooking, and some childcare while Sonia was teaching. At the time, she was teaching classes for servicemen, diplomats, and their wives and children and had little responsibility at home. She "saw how men can grow when they have someone to take over the drudgery of living, turn their attention to work. How exhilarating that is!"[19] In Korea, Sonia could focus on her own work, her own growth, and her own self. Soon, though, the family moved from Korea to Malaysia, where Sonia gave birth to her fourth and last child, Noel, in a relatively easy birth. She became profoundly depressed. She missed her teaching work and had "only the children between me and total uselessness again."[20] Full-time motherhood no longer agreed with her.

When the Johnsons returned to the United States in 1974, they spent another year in Palo Alto. Rick quickly became restless with his job at Stanford, so the next year, he accepted a position with the U.S. Department of Education that required that he travel around the country. The Johnsons spent the next year living and traveling in an RV. After that, they settled in Sterling, Virginia, where they purchased their first home in June 1976. Before the Johnsons settled in Virginia, Sonia did not consider herself a feminist and mostly thought herself a rather typical Mormon housewife who spent most of her time caring for a home and children. In Virginia, Sonia came to feminism reluctantly through a series of minor and major epiphanies.

Feminist Awakenings

When the Johnsons returned to the United States in 1976, they found a country beset by the women's movement. Inspired by the Black freedom movement and other movements that characterized the "new left," the U.S. women's
movement began in the 1960s as Americans began to question long-standing
gender ideals that relegated women (primarily white, middle-class women)
to raising children in the home, while men participated more broadly in
the fullness of human experience. Over the middle and late 1970s, feminist
activism became increasingly captured by the campaign for the ERA. The
National Organization for Women (NOW), the preeminent feminist lobbying
organization in the nation, came to the forefront of the public movement, and
more radical organizations and sectors of the movement were progressively
more and more marginalized.[21] A constitutional amendment must pass both
houses of Congress by a two-thirds majority and then be ratified by the vote
of the state legislatures of three-fourths of U.S. states (a total of thirty-eight
states). The ERA passed Congress quickly and twenty-two states ratified it
in 1972. Five more joined in early 1973. Mid-decade, a fierce battle broke out,
and between 1974 and 1977, only five additional states approved the ERA while
five others attempted to rescind their ratification.

The women's movement had implications for LDS culture.[22] In Boston,
Massachusetts, a group of women, including Mormon women's history
notables Claudia Bushman and Laurel Thatcher Ulrich, began meeting
to discuss their lives as Mormon women. The group published an issue
of *Dialogue: A Journal of Mormon Thought* and a book titled *Mormon
Sisters: Women in Early Utah*, devoted to early Mormon women's history.
In 1974, they started a newsletter they named *Exponent II* in homage to
the early Mormon women's newspaper, *Woman's Exponent*. "Poised on the
dual platforms of Mormonism and Feminism," the first issue of *Exponent
II* came out in July 1974.[23] Within a year, subscriptions had outstripped any
of the founders' expectations, reaching four thousand by simple word of
mouth. *Exponent II* has since become the longest-running periodical for
LDS women in history. Although each issue included at least one article
with a feminist viewpoint, the paper was "by no means militant."[24] No one in
the group faced church discipline for their activities. Decades after the first
issue of *Exponent II* emerged, historian Jan Shipps said that the publication

avoided church leaders' notice by simply providing a platform for many varied LDS women's voices rather than taking any particular positions.[25]

Closer to church headquarters in Salt Lake City, controversy erupted over the women's movement in 1977. In response to the United Nations' declaration of International Women's Year (IWY) in 1975, individual U.S. states held IWY conventions. LDS feminist Jan Tyler organized the Utah IWY convention. She had planned for three thousand participants, but in June 1977, well over thirteen thousand women swarmed the Utah conference, many of them LDS women with instructions "to attend the conference as a ward representative, to vote down the ERA and other feminist resolutions."[26]

Sonia was either out of the country or traveling with Rick and their children in a motor home for most of this time, so she did not keep up on the activities of the Boston feminists. Neither did she take note of the debacle that unfolded in Salt Lake City except in retrospect. Although Sonia sometimes drew on some of the history uncovered by the group in Boston, especially the early Mormon *Woman's Exponent*, her feminism took a much different path than either the Boston group or LDS feminists in Salt Lake City. Her frame of reference was more the national women's movement, especially as it was embodied in the late 1970s by the battle over the ERA, than Mormon feminism represented by the likes of *Exponent II*.

In Virginia, Sonia and Rick reconnected with good friends from graduate school, Ron and Hazel Rigby. Hazel introduced Sonia to the women's movement. Conversations between Sonia and Hazel "began to open up a whole new and frightening in a sense—well, it wasn't frightening, it was just . . . painful—world to me, and that's the world of women. I realize now I had been a male-oriented, male-identified woman all my life. . . . And that I had therefore spent most of my time in that effort to please them."[27] These exchanges, alongside her earlier rather modest feminist moments, primed Sonia's move into feminism, and she didn't go easily: "Every single inch forward was painful to me."[28] Always a voracious reader, Sonia began reading in the then-burgeoning field of feminist theory. As she read, she became increasingly depressed. In good LDS fashion, she prayed to ask God to

> tell me, what is the thing that I have been hiding from myself and that I simply must now face or die? And then I heard my voice, my own personal voice, say . . . loudly and clearly, "patriarchy is a sham." Well, I

understood immediately why I hadn't wanted to know that. My whole life was built on . . . the belief that patriarchy was God-archy, was God's plan, God's way. And it undercut one of the basic traditions and beliefs of the Mormon church, and of my life. And I plunged—although I hadn't thought it would be possible—I plunged from black despair to total utter complete terror.[29]

This seems to have been the most powerful of Sonia's feminist stirrings before her epiphanic conversion to the ERA in 1977.

In October 1976, only a few months after the Johnsons moved to Virginia, the First Presidency of the church issued its first official statement in opposition to the ERA. At the time, Sonia considered herself "mildly pro-ERA" and envisioned her primary role as a traditional Mormon housewife and mother of four children.[30] A few months later, Sonia began hearing about the ERA from the pulpit during church services. For her, confronting the church's anti-ERA political position during church meetings interrupted and encroached on her ability to worship, experience fellowship, and receive sacred instruction in peace. She watched her weekly religious meeting change midstream "to a precinct meeting."[31] She would later say, "You don't belong to church because of its political beliefs. . . . You belong to it because you believe in the doctrine, because that's where you get your spiritual nourishment. It shouldn't be a political organization."[32] Seeking an intelligent discussion on what drove the church's politics, Sonia invited some friends, including Hazel, to join her at a meeting in April 1977 at which local authorities promised to explain the church's position on the ERA. In the meeting, a local church leader began by announcing that he knew nothing about the ERA, so he had stopped at the 7-Eleven store on the way to the meeting and purchased a copy of *Pageant* magazine (a women's monthly) to learn.[33] He read the magazine article during the opening song and prayer and then proceeded to tell the women why they should oppose the ERA. Sometime during the meeting, the speaker read the ERA aloud and changed Sonia's life forever. The ERA "just took a hold of my heart right then. And it hasn't let go for one single second, waking or sleeping since. I don't understand why."[34]

Sonia walked out of the meeting completely incensed: "I was so angry that there isn't a word in the men's dictionary for it. I mean rage is a puny little word. Fury is just sickly, totally. All of them are inadequate, and all of them together can never begin to express this feeling of just wanting to

"Patriarchy Is a Sham"

blow apart."[35] She was enraged that she had encouraged pro-ERA friends to drive for over an hour and the speaker hadn't bothered to learn anything about the issue until five minutes before the meeting. Sonia and her friends in attendance "had come hungering and thirsting after help. . . . We needed somebody to have some compassion and some understanding and help us with this, oh my word. It was brutal to watch this man stand up there and say he hadn't prepared anything." For Sonia, this demonstrated "how trivial [church leaders] thought women's issues were." Had the presentation been about men's constitutional rights, Sonia argued, the speaker certainly would have been better prepared. Instead, "we got *Pageant*," a women's magazine Sonia rather generously called "a C-grade *Readers Digest*."[36]

Sonia credits this event with her most significant and most painful feminist epiphany, an event she later called "the bursting of the file." In *Housewife to Heretic*, she claimed that somewhere in each women's mind is "a unique file entitled 'What it means to be female in a male world.'" Women add the data of their experiences to the file, though with varying degrees of awareness, and then finally, "there comes along the one piece of data that breaks it wide open."[37] For Sonia, that piece of data was *Pageant* magazine. Sonia returned home from the meeting and locked herself in a room above the garage away from the rest of the family and shouted and raged at God for hours. She told Him how angry and betrayed and humiliated she was that she had loved and trusted Him. She told God that women's confinement under patriarchy "was the most vicious, the ugliest, and ultimately the most evil thing that had ever been done, and that if I could get a hold of him I would kill him."[38] So began Sonia's confrontation with the LDS church and life's work as a women's liberation thinker and advocate. After this epiphany, a series of events I chronicle more thoroughly in chapter 2 culminated in Sonia's excommunication from the church she loved deeply and in which five generations of her family had lived their lives. It took less than three years for her to travel from housewife to heretic.

Sonia's Public Feminism

In July 1978, Sonia marched with other women in a demonstration in Washington, D.C. supporting the extension of the deadline for passage of the ERA by state legislatures, carrying a banner that read "Mormons for ERA." Together with her friends Hazel Rigby, Maida Withers, and Teddie Wood,

Sonia cofounded the organization Mormons for ERA (MERA). In August, when the bill to extend the time to pass the ERA had passed the House of Representatives and went to the Senate, Sonia made her first public appearance as a Mormon feminist. She testified before the U.S. Senate Judiciary Committee on the Constitution, Civil Rights, and Property Rights in support of the ERA. Apparently, she was invited to appear because someone on the staff of Indiana senator Birch Bayh, who initiated the hearings, had remembered the "Mormons for ERA" sign from the recent protest and contacted Sonia. After some sleepless nights of anxiety, Sonia, a well-educated Mormon housewife with no official church authority at all, testified for the ERA alongside a Catholic priest, a rabbi, and a United Presbyterian minister. Sonia's five-minute speech quoted nineteenth-century LDS women equal rights activists who, with the full support of church leadership, had advocated for woman suffrage and women's rights. (She may have come into contact with this history through her relationships with LDS liberals in Palo Alto.) Surely, she claimed, these same women would now support the ERA.

During the question-and-answer period, Sonia and Utah Republican senator Orrin Hatch had a fiery exchange covered by news outlets around the country. Hatch said, "Mrs. Johnson, you must admit that nearly 100 percent of Mormon women oppose the Equal Rights Amendment." Sonia retorted, "Oh my goodness, I don't have to admit that. It simply isn't true." The banter continued for a short time until Hatch lost his temper. He banged his fists angrily on the table as he nearly shouted his last sentence, "It's implied by your testimony that you're more intelligent than other Mormon women, and that if they were all as intelligent as you, they would support the Equal Rights Amendment. Now that's an insult to my wife!"[39]

This exchange woke up the sleepy press corps covering the event. At its end, Sonia found herself speaking into microphones and tape recorders of reporters from the Associated Press, United Press International, and Knight Ridder. Newspapers in the region wrote about the exchange.[40] In those interviews, Sonia discovered a hidden talent: she was a master at captivating the press and exploiting its political potential. Sonia received a multitude of letters of gratitude and support in the wake of this appearance, primarily from pro-ERA church members who had been struggling in isolation with the church's position. A bit tongue in cheek, Sonia took many public speaking opportunities to credit Hatch's hostile and condescending outburst for the national success of MERA.[41]

MERA was more of a mailing list than a formal organization, but its founders were devoted to exposing the covert activity of the LDS church against the ERA. Sonia did not have paid employment at the time and the other three founders did, so Sonia took on the bulk of the public work, while others managed the bank account, edited the newsletter, and worked behind the scenes. Sonia became the most recognized public face of MERA and of LDS feminism until the ERA was defeated in June 1982. In October 1978, two months after Sonia's Senate testimony, the First Presidency of the LDS church sent a letter read aloud in every congregation urging church members "to join actively with other citizens who share our concerns and who are engaged in working to reject this measure on the basis of its threat to the moral climate of the future."[42] Local leaders and members in many states, especially those still unratified, took seriously this call to political activism. They followed a pattern first established in 1977 in Nevada.[43] Church regional representatives called on leaders of the Relief Society, the church's women's organization, to serve as "key coordinators" in organizing the women of their congregations against the ERA.[44] Events in Virginia in response to this call to activism are especially important because Sonia lived in Virginia, so those events framed and shaped broader discussions between church representatives and Sonia and her supporters.

In November 1978, an article in the Oakton, Virginia *Stake Newsletter*, a small mimeographed publication from Sonia's stake (a collection of wards), claimed that LDS church president Spencer W. Kimball had asked regional representatives Julian Lowe and Don Ladd to organize the women of the region to campaign against the ERA, though it was likely Gordon B. Hinckley who carried the message.[45] Lowe and Ladd held a meeting to found the organization that would become the Virginia LDS Citizens Coalition (VACC). As I discuss more thoroughly in chapter 2, this meeting was in many ways representative of the central disagreements about LDS anti-ERA activity at the core of Sonia's campaign against the LDS church. She frequently quoted (and misquoted) statements from this meeting as evidence for her larger claims about the church's activism. LDS women's coalitions in other states used the VACC organization as a model for their own groups, and Sonia likewise used the church's political activity in Virginia as a paradigmatic basis for many of her criticisms of LDS anti-ERA activism.

Sonia's form of activism is best characterized as anti-anti-ERA, rather than pro-ERA. To her, the church's anti-ERA activism felt like dirty pool, and she was determined to expose it. As she told one interviewer, "I just want the church out of politics, or if it is in politics, I want it to play honestly."[46] After her Senate speech, Sonia was often invited by state or regional chapters of NOW or by other pro-ERA organizations, especially in unratified states, to help them combat the LDS church's campaigns against the ERA in their area. At these meetings and in her press and other public appearances, Sonia exposed the clandestine ways the church was recruiting its members, raising funds, and using church buildings and other resources to campaign against the ERA. She saw this work as advancing the church: "I always felt it was beneficial for the church to be exposed. If we can stop them from doing really dubious kinds of political stuff, that's a help to the church."[47] Especially controversial, in April 1979, MERA flew a banner over the semiannual General Conference of the LDS church in Salt Lake City reading, "Mormons for ERA Are Everywhere," which received front-page coverage in the *Salt Lake Tribune* and merited a short article in the *Los Angeles Times*.[48] MERA flew several banners over church events over the next few years. From late 1978 through June 1982, Sonia and her compatriots engaged in various forms of activism, sometimes outlandish and often humorous, many of which received coverage in newspapers across the country. She also spoke widely. The effect of most of these actions was precisely what Sonia intended: they focused public attention on the LDS church's campaign against the ERA.[49]

Sonia's activism and the sensationalized drama of her excommunication, alongside her eloquence and charm, made her a national political and media sensation. Her excommunication and activism made national headlines for months, informing a curious American public about Mormonism and its national activism in opposition to the ERA. Especially in the months surrounding her excommunication, discussion of the "family feud" between Sonia and the LDS church inundated the press and Sonia became a household name. As the threat of excommunication loomed, press coverage of Sonia's predicament increased, especially in Utah, Virginia, and nearby Washington, D.C., and coverage of the drama overtook coverage of the church's campaigns against the ERA. Letters to the editor discussing Sonia's situation flooded into local newspapers. This notoriety sometimes brought Sonia into contact with other LDS feminists, especially those in Salt Lake City, some of whom she established meaningful friendships with.[50] She remained on the national radar for the next few years in part because in November 1981, she published a memoir of her experience,

14

From Housewife to Heretic. The book clarifies much of what distinguished Sonia from other Mormon feminists of the time and much of what made her excommunication so controversial in the Mormon community. She had no interest in diluting her feminism to accommodate more moderate LDS perspectives or in welcoming a diversity of LDS women's perspectives and was willing to critique in public and visible ways the male authority and family relationships on which LDS theology is based. Within one month, the memoir was ninth on the *New York Times* bestsellers list.[51]

In the LDS church, excommunication is the most severe disciplinary action that excises an individual from church membership, nullifies eternal marriage and family relationships, and cuts off access to God's blessings.[52] Although formally understood as "a court of love" that offers members an opportunity to repent, members who are excommunicated are no longer a member of the LDS community and the experience is often experienced as punitive and unkind. Resulting social and spiritual censure can be quite callous.

As I discuss at length in chapter 2, after two trial meetings totaling around seven hours, Sonia was excommunicated from the LDS church on December 5, 1979, by her bishop, Jeffrey Willis. Sonia has always maintained, as have many other observers, that she was excommunicated for her pro-ERA activism or, more specifically, for her activism in exposing and opposing the LDS church's anti-ERA activities. Church representatives have always disputed this interpretation, claiming instead that Sonia harmed church programs (especially the missionary program), publicly criticized church leadership, falsely accused the church of imposing the prophet's moral directives on the nation, and was generally out of alignment with church teachings. In the months following her excommunication, church representatives also said that Sonia had taught false doctrine and publicly criticized church authorities and programs.

Days before or within a few weeks after her excommunication, Sonia's story was featured on nearly every nationally syndicated talk and news shows including the *Today* show and the *Tomorrow* show with Tom Snyder. She appeared as a solo guest on *Donahue* and several local radio and television talk shows across the country. Outside the church building the day of her excommunication, she spoke with reporters from the *New York Times*, the *Washington Post*, CBS, NBC, PBS, *People*, *Newsweek*, and *Time* magazines, and most major news organizations. The day after her excommunication, the story appeared in over six hundred fifty newspapers across the United States. Sonia welcomed media attention, while church representatives refused to speak with reporters. Over the first months of 1980, Sonia appealed the decision first to her stake president, Earl Roueche, and then to Church President Spencer W. Kimball. Both appeals were widely reported in the press, and both were denied.

Although not publicly known until mid-January 1980, while her excommunication was proceeding, Sonia also underwent a very painful break with her husband, Rick, though he continued to support her during and after her excommunication. When it became public, the divorce perhaps obliged Sonia to talk more publicly about her personal life than she was comfortable with, and her political activism disguised to the public (and perhaps to Sonia herself) the magnitude of the personal tragedy. Nonetheless, a few days after Sonia was excommunicated, Rick requested in solidarity to have his name removed from the records of the church. Rick's request, widely publicized in the press, said that he was "shocked at the savage misogyny you demonstrated during the trial and since. . . . Your entire case in Bishop's Court was based on a few of Sonia's statements quoted out of context and incorrectly as well (as the testimony showed), and you gave a dishonest account of what happened in the trial in your press statement."[53] The church obliged and removed Rick's name from its membership records.

A few months after Sonia appeared on Tom Snyder's show, a producer at the show asked church spokesperson Charlie Gibbs why church leaders had refused to meet with Sonia. In response, Gibbs arranged a private, off-the-record meeting between Gordon B. Hinckley, Neal A. Maxwell, both members of the Special Affairs Committee (SAC), and Sonia and her friend Jan Tyler. Sonia remembered Hinckley and Maxwell repeatedly humiliating the two women and trivializing the ERA. She claimed that Hinckley told her that the SAC was the least important thing he did and feigned ignorance of the anti-ERA organizations he had instigated. The meeting confirmed Sonia's suspicion that the problem was not church leaders' ignorance about the issues; it was that church leaders had no interest in listening to or caring about women. Ultimately, they "didn't hear it at all. They don't know what women in pain even means." When Sonia left that meeting, "my fighting spirit was up, boy. I said to myself, those men can now be fought with impunity. . . . We don't have to worry that perhaps they really are decent, and they just don't understand. . . . They cannot understand."[54] Sonia would continue to fight against the church and for the ERA until its defeat in June 1982.

"Patriarchy Is a Sham"

16

The few years before and after Sonia's excommunication were a bit of a whirlwind for her, leaving her little time for contemplation or deep reflection on her experiences. Sonia's memoir, *From Housewife to Heretic*, has moments of reflection embedded within the narrative but does not present a systematic application of experience to a broader feminist analysis. Points in the narrative illustrate and critique men's assumption and exercise of power over women, the sexual double standard, women's internalization of patriarchy, men's patriarchal alliances with each other, and other features of patriarchy. Much of Sonia's more holistic feminist worldview came later in her life as she made sense of the experiences she had during these years and after. Between 1978 and 1982, she was having many of the experiences that would shape her later feminism. In her estimation, she watched male LDS leaders conspire against her and against women's rights, she saw men lying to women repeatedly, and she saw women internalizing patriarchy and following men's leadership without question. But these experiences came too fast and too hard for careful consideration.

In the months following her excommunication, Sonia also came to terms with her divorce. She believed that before her feminist awakening, Rick had been the center of her life. As she tells it, after she began her ERA activism, the ERA replaced Rick at the center of her life, so Rick found someone else. In *Housewife to Heretic*, Sonia declared that "no man can ever be my center."[55] Sonia became a lesbian after the defeat of the ERA "finally disillusioned me about men" and has lived a life surrounded by and devoted to women ever since.[56]

Sonia's Feminism after Excommunication

Sonia's confrontation with the church and the notoriety that came with it shaped her subsequent life in many ways. Through it, she developed tremendous courage, barely blinking an eye while speaking before the U.S. Senate, talking to reporter after reporter on national news broadcasts and for national and local news outlets, and appearing several times on national and local talk and news radio and television shows. After her excommunication, Sonia was in high demand as a public speaker, giving hundreds of speeches over the next several years. She spoke at the 1980 Democratic National Convention in support of the ERA, leading the crowd in an enthusiastic ERA chant.[57]

Sonia's relationship to NOW and its leadership became increasingly vexed over the early 1980s. The main tension was over the forms and philosophy of political activism. While NOW embodied fairly accommodationist activism, working with men and within American political systems, Sonia became increasingly committed to a more confrontational style. Her experience with the church had taught her that men could not be reasoned with and would never simply "give" women their rights. Rights must be seized. Sonia came to see civil disobedience as the most meaningful political strategy for women, arguing that no social movement had ever succeeded without it.[58]

Her acts of civil disobedience sometimes made national headlines. She argued that women, like the founding fathers of the United States, must be prepared to die for their political rights. She wrote in 1981 that "the only appropriate feeling for women in the United States today is rage and the only appropriate action is immoderation."[59] She demonstrated at LDS temples and churches, the Republican National Convention, the White House, and other high- and low-profile locations and events. In one especially well-publicized event, she and twenty other women protested outside the gates of the LDS temple in Bellevue, Washington (a suburb of Seattle), some chaining themselves to the fence. The "Bellevue 21," as they came to be called, were arrested, and one protester sued a temple official for assault because he had pushed her to the ground during the confrontation.[60] Sonia was arrested again when she helped stage a sit-in for the ERA that blocked traffic in front of the White House.

In October 1981, a group of women Sonia brought together organized a civil disobedience workshop as part of the program of the national NOW conference in Washington, D.C. Sonia reports that when hundreds of women showed up to the civil disobedience workshop, the concurrent "speak out" session organized by NOW leaders was nearly empty. The fallout from this event was that NOW leaders polarized NOW members into an "either NOW or Sonia" dichotomy and intimidated attendees of the civil disobedience conference into silence.[61] At this conference, Sonia felt that "NOW was using the same methods of intimidation and fear to control their group that I had watched the Elders use all my life in the Church."[62] When NOW leaders called Sonia to their hotel room to confront her, she thought, "I haven't been in a meeting like this since I was in the Mormon Church."[63] For Sonia, NOW's accommodationist politics had made the organization into the very thing it opposed: a hierarchical organization modeled on patriarchy, just like the LDS church.

As the ERA neared its final defeat, Sonia joined six other women in a thirty-seven-day fast in the Illinois capitol building under a banner that read, "Women Fast for Justice." Illinois was the last state whose ratification could have pushed the number of ratified states to the required thirty-eight. The fasters stopped only after the defeat of the ERA was absolute, and by then, Sonia was confined to a wheelchair and another demonstrator had been hospitalized. The defeat of the ERA by the Illinois legislature on June 30, 1982, marked the end of any realistic hope of passing the ERA. It also convinced Sonia that it was useless to try to convince men to bestow rights on women, even through civil disobedience. She quickly came to see that the utility of civil disobedience was not to oppose men but to build women's courage so that other women could see women fighting for them.

In the fall of 1982, just after the defeat of the ERA, Sonia ran for president of NOW. She saw herself as embarking on "an aggressive campaign to try ... to turn NOW into a feminist organization, instead of merely a women's civil rights organization."[64] That is, she hoped to reverse the trend by which NOW was becoming more conventional and patriarchal and, in her mind, less committed to the feminist principles of nonhierarchy and radical egalitarianism. At stake in the campaign was nothing less than the direction of the entire organization. Sonia wanted less hierarchy, a more democratic and diffused leadership model, a commitment to civil disobedience, and a withdrawal from participation in politics as usual. By her account, "the other candidates stood for reform and white gloves and making the men respect us."[65] In a bitterly contested election, Sonia lost to Judy Goldsmith. The loss convinced her that NOW had become irretrievably patriarchal, so she and many of her supporters broke ties with the organization. During the NOW presidential campaign, Sonia struggled with a body weakened from the ERA fast, motherhood, and a general sense of overwhelm. She sought out a feminist counselor and a friend introduced her to Susan Horwitz. Within a year, Sonia and Horwitz became lesbian partners and Horwitz had become Sonia's press secretary.

Following Sonia's failed campaign for the presidency of NOW, her politics moved in two mutually contradictory directions. As she discusses in her second book, *Going Out of Our Minds*, she became increasingly disenchanted with the public institutions of government, the political sphere, and anything that smacked of politics as usual, believing that using "male-identified" forms of power to accomplish women's ends compromised the essence of feminism. Instead, these efforts made women themselves more male defined and as patriarchal as the forces they opposed. Opposing patriarchy makes women its unwitting accomplices—"What we resist persists," she was fond of saying.[66] In this sense, Sonia withdrew from engaging with patriarchal politics as usual, and instead, in the summers of 1983 and 1984, she facilitated "woman gatherings" at which attendees tried to create "woman's culture" apart from patriarchy. She also grew increasingly critical of men as a class, though in her terms, she was not a man-hater, merely a teller of the truth about men.[67]

At the same time, Sonia did perhaps the most hierarchical, most male-defined, most patriarchal thing anyone could imagine—she ran for president of the United States in 1984. Her campaign was affiliated with the Citizen's Party, the Peace and Freedom Party of California, and the Consumer Party in Pennsylvania and ran under the slogan "A Woman for a Change."[68] Her platform emphasized unilateral disarmament, women's voices in government, an end to violence against women and the environment, and the waging of peace.[69] Sonia ran not to win, for she believed that political campaigns can be instruments of change only "when candidates have no expectations of winning—and no desire for victory."[70] Rather, Sonia ran so that women could see her running, to encourage women to take themselves seriously without men's permission by doing so herself.[71] Perhaps more important, she hoped her campaign would change the "morphogenetic field, the entire global paradigm" of politics itself, "replacing with life giving values the decayed and crumbling foundations of the fathers' failed experiment."[72] Sonia received almost seventy-two thousand votes.

After her presidential run, Sonia continued to make a living public speaking at universities, feminist organizations, and other places. At the same time, she became even more dissatisfied with the more personal dynamics of patriarchy: family, motherhood, sex, and intimacy. Even though she dedicated her 1989 book to her daughter, Kari, Sonia increasingly took aim at the forces that structured women's personal lives. In her 1989 book *Wildfire*, she called motherhood "the last taboo" and declared that she had found motherhood "most unsatisfactory."[73] In particular, she had found it difficult to watch her three sons come to despise the feminine in themselves and to assert male privilege as patriarchy demanded.[74] She advocated that women take control of mothering and do something—anything—different to reclaim it for themselves. She had come to see her own years of mothering as an "empty, loveless time. . . . All I learned from it was how to endure pain."[75]

Along the way, Sonia's relationship with Susan Horwitz ended and she had a second lesbian relationship with a woman named Chris. Sonia described Chris as "very sexual," and Sonia did not enjoy sex. Within a few years of this relationship, she published a book arguing that sex was inherently a patriarchal act. Probably in 1989, as this second lesbian relationship was also ending, Sonia woke up with a sore knee. An acquaintance told her of a feminist herbalist clinic in Ojo Caliente, New Mexico. There, she met Jade DeForest, who was working at the clinic. Jade treated Sonia's knee and the two became fast friends.

During this time, Sonia also abandoned her public speaking career partly because demand dried up but also because she "didn't want to be a big deal and all these women in my audience little deals. . . . It went against everything in me to do that."[76] She has since maintained a clear contempt for hierarchy in any and all forms. Instead, she turned her efforts to trying to enact alternative, nonpatriarchal, nonhierarchical ways of living she had theorized in her 1989 book. Sonia and several lesbian friends, including Jade, purchased a run-down monastery in the mountains near Albuquerque, New Mexico and rebuilt it. There, they established a short-lived feminist community. Within a few years, the community unraveled amid personal and financial scandal; participants accused Sonia of authoritarian leadership and of mishandling community finances.[77] Sonia, however, blamed the failure of this and all women's communities on women's inability to escape patriarchal consciousness.[78] After everyone had left the monastery except Sonia and Jade, the two fell in love and decided to combine their lives.

Around the same time, Sonia decided to become a nonmother. She purchased her children, the youngest now seventeen years old, a house and then told them, "You never call me, never write me, never send messages to me through anyone. Never get in touch with me again. The minute you do, I am a mother again, and I really can't bear it."[79] Sonia's public writings say that she did this in part out of disdain for the hierarchy of parent-child relationships but also to reclaim herself and her life back from the role of motherhood. She told an interviewer in 2010 that "motherhood is a role.

It's not a person. . . . I can't be a role anymore."[80] She could at last be "not a wife, not a mother, not a daughter," simply herself.[81] Sonia had come to see motherhood as an irreversible form of entrapment to the role of "mother."[82] More recently, Sonia told me that by the time she made this decision, she simply didn't like her three sons. Two of them had impregnated girls in high school, and one had become "such a misogynist." They taught her that despite her attempts to turn them into feminists, "you can't make men understand. You can't make them want to understand." She had also realized that her relationship with Jade was incompatible with motherhood because it "makes you into the kind of person that Jade wouldn't be able to tolerate," so she had chosen Jade over motherhood.[83]

In the mid-1990s, soon after selling the monastery, Sonia grew even more weary of the notoriety that continued to follow her, especially in feminist circles. Seeking a low-profile life, she briefly went by Jade's last name, moved with Jade to Arizona, and worked in a hardware store. The two then returned to New Mexico in 2007, where they opened a women's motel called Casa Feminista. There, women could experience women's community in small doses. After the motel closed, Sonia and Jade lived briefly in a women's community in Georgia and then returned to Arizona.

Most recently, Sonia has appeared in interviews and appearances with excommunicated LDS feminist Kate Kelly.[84] She also appeared in a 2018 television program reuniting Sonia with one of her fellow ERA fasters, Zoe Nicholson.[85] In 2019, Sonia wrote her most recent publication, a four-page epilogue to the second edition of Nicholson's published diary of the fast, *The Hungry Heart: A Woman's Fast for Justice*.[86] In it, Sonia affirms women's "destiny to create out of our magnificent female souls an entirely opposite universal community, one as potently loving, creative, and beneficent as theirs [men's] has been weak, destructive, and maleficent."[87] As of June 2023, Sonia, now eighty-seven years old, nourishes her hope for such a world, though at times encounters deep despair at its failure to arrive, in a quiet life with Jade in southern Arizona.

CHAPTER TWO

"Well, I'm About to Find Out"
Disciplining Mormons, Disciplining Feminism

Just before Sonia Johnson's excommunication, Diane Sawyer asked her on the nationally syndicated talk show if she could be both a Mormon and a feminist. Sonia responded, "Well, I'm about to find out."[1] As Utah reporter Linda Sillitoe claimed shortly after Sonia's excommunication, "In the Sonia Johnson story, oversimplification is the lie."[2] This chapter tells the story of Sonia's excommunication in at least some of its complexity, with an eye to how it illustrates issues of gender, authority, belief, and control that emerged among Mormons in the wake of the women's movement. The fact that Sonia's dramatic confrontation with the church played out on a national stage significantly increased the stakes—for Sonia, for the church, and for LDS women.

The disciplinary effects of Sonia's excommunication on other LDS feminists indicate that her experience had implications much broader than her membership in the church. Sonia thought of and widely discussed her excommunication not only as a personal tragedy but also as a microcosm for the situation of LDS women more broadly. She saw the process she endured as revealing of male leaders' control of LDS women and of the moral and political danger of the church's anti-ERA campaigns: just as church leaders tried to control Sonia's public activism with religious censure, church patriarchy exercised control over women generally; just as Sonia's excommunication was unjust and unkind, so were the church's unfair and unethical political tactics.

Sonia's excommunication has meant many different things to many different people. In one sense, the story of Sonia's excommunication was as the press at the time framed it, a story of one lone woman struggling against and eventually losing to a much more powerful church priesthood hierarchy. In another sense, church leaders' "witch hunt," as Sonia termed it, was also an exercise in the gendered power of male church leaders to define the terms and meaning of her public statements as they deliberately used and misquoted her words against her. Sonia was a woman gaining public influence in opposition to patriarchal church leaders. Relative to her excommunication, though, the hermeneutical power of priesthood leaders prevailed over her own. Yet if Sonia failed at exercising her own power, she could at least expose the damage done to women by the men of the church. She could use the press to expose their anti-ERA activism; she could be an example to other LDS women wanting to speak out in opposition to the church's anti-ERA position; and she could, through her own excommunication, expose the men of the church as "the fiends that they are."[3]

At the core of Sonia's conflict with the church were more complex questions about the disciplining force of church leadership and of religion more broadly. Her excommunication crystallized these larger questions in a microcosm of her life. Sonia's story illustrates how, in the case of the ERA, the threat of church discipline worked as a patriarchal and uniquely Mormon way of containing and controlling the opinions and activism of ordinary church members while also shaping and policing believers' overall gender and family conservativism. That is, Sonia's excommunication confirmed for some believers the excesses of feminism, but for others, it suppressed feminist dissent.

Implicit and sometimes explicit in Sonia's critiques were broader criticisms of LDS patriarchal priesthood writ large. One of the church's founding principles is the patriarchal order of the priesthood. In the LDS church, all worthy males over the age of twelve hold some level of priesthood power, defined by the LDS church as the power of God. Priesthood ordination is a prerequisite for almost all governing and policymaking positions in the church. Whether Mormonism's founding prophet, Joseph Smith, originally intended a priesthood only of men is contested.[4] Yet the body of the church has been governed by male priesthood holders, while women have governed women's and children's organizations. Since the 1960s at the latest, they have done so under the supervision of male priesthood holders.

As feminists in the twentieth century have pressed toward equality with men and challenged the very nature and necessity of gender altogether, the maleness of church governance has come increasingly under attack, primarily from feminist directions. While Sonia was not the first to critique priesthood leadership on the grounds of gender, she was the first to do so from within the church in a wide-scale nationally visible way and with the support of a powerful national feminist movement. The debate within the church over the ERA was arguably the first time that contests within the church over gender and power came to national attention, shaping both Americans' understandings of Mormonism and Mormons' understandings of themselves.

Although it is difficult to say for certain why the press was so captivated by Sonia's situation, her notoriety was at least in part her own making. Sonia actively courted press attention in ways some observers found self-involved. She showed a natural ability to manage and even embrace her notoriety and was startlingly unfazed by the very public character of her life during those years. She also had a fine sense of humor and a clever and sometimes biting wit. As Linda Sillitoe remarked, Sonia "favors a vivid word over a bland word every time." There was "a more noticeable discrepancy between her words in print and her words as heard than is usually noticeable," and "her use of hyperbole and sometimes startlingly vivid language is usually humorous or ironic, but when she speaks from pain . . . her rhetoric strikes many Mormons as polemic and harsh."[5] She was also incredibly warm, witty, articulate, and charming, and she had a talent for engaging with the press, though she could be uncompromising and sometimes blinded by the totality of her commitment to the ERA. In a moment of self-awareness, she told Patrick Greenlaw, for example, that "I am such a single-issue person that I scare myself to death."[6] Sonia's provocative style seemed to have emerged out of nowhere within 1970s Mormonism—she was a true anomaly. However, her notoriety also benefited from the historical moment at which she burst onto the national stage. As a result of renewed opposition to the ERA over the latter 1970s, particularly from the likes of Phyllis Schlafly's StopERA organization, public debate over the ERA escalated. Sonia emerged in 1978 as a new and dynamic feminist from a church firmly rooted in conservative opposition, and the specter of a lone woman standing for the ERA against her patriarchal church made for an engaging drama.

LDS Anti-ERA Activism

LDS anti-ERA activism preconditioned Sonia's activism against the church and her excommunication from it. One of the most difficult aspects of writing about both the church's anti-ERA campaign and the excommunication of Sonia is the question of accountability. At times, the terms "church representatives," "church leaders," or "the First Presidency" are not entirely accurate or known assignments of responsibility, especially in a culture in which implication, allusion, and common understanding can sometimes direct behavior as effectively as direct instruction or command. In these instances, the very vagueness of the term "the church" is what makes it the most accurate—frequently, who exactly within the church was articulating a position or directing members' behavior was unclear. In some instances, this opacity was central to Sonia's criticisms—it allowed church leaders to avoid accountability for their behavior.

Church opposition to the ERA was evident by the mid-1970s, and it mattered. It shaped members' opinions and propelled many of them to unprecedented political activism. The ERA was introduced to Congress in 1972, and within a few years, church notables such as Relief Society presidents Belle Stafford and Barbara Smith spoke publicly against it.[7] LDS opposition appeared with more institutional backing when an unsigned editorial in the *Church News* appeared in January 1975, a few weeks before the Utah state legislature convened for the year with plans to vote on the ERA. The editorial argued that the ERA's blanket approach "would work to the disadvantage of both women and men." It emphasized that each gender "has his or her role" and expressed concern that the ERA would be a "unisex" law. Besides, it said, legislation already existed to provide women with "statutory equality."[8] The *Deseret News* reported that before the January 1975 *Church News* editorial, over 65 percent of Utah favored the amendment;[9] a month later, only around 40 percent did. When results were narrowed to only LDS respondents, support declined sharply from 63 percent to 31 percent over the same month.[10] The Utah legislature voted against ratifying the ERA a few weeks after the *Church News* editorial appeared.

Three more official church statements against the ERA appeared over the signature of the First Presidency in October 1976, August 1978, and October 1978. In March 1980, three months after Sonia's excommunication, the church produced its most thorough discussion of its anti-ERA position in a pamphlet titled *The Church and the Proposed Equal Rights Amendment: A Moral Issue* (commonly known as the Gray Book). The twenty-three-page booklet was mailed with every March issue of the church magazine, *The Ensign*, and was otherwise widely distributed among members, especially in unratified states. It reprinted all three of the First Presidency's official statements against the ERA and carried with it the implicit endorsement of church leaders. It also added a more thorough set of legal arguments to the moral concerns the church had already expressed. That same year, two pamphlets, titled *Why Mormon Women Oppose the ERA* and *The Equal Rights Dilemma*, were printed with church funds (but not identified as such) and widely distributed to church members inside and outside church buildings in several states.[11]

The church's moral claims stipulated that the ERA threatened marriage, gender norms and relations, children, and families in four primary ways. First, the ERA would weaken the family because it would "stifle many God-given feminine instincts."[12] Church leaders were unclear about what these were, but based on other church publications from the time, those "instincts" related to bearing and raising children.[13] Second, the church argued that the ERA would nullify benefits that accrued to women based on differences "biologically, emotionally, and in other ways."[14] These included special protections awarded to women as child bearers, such as protections for pregnant women in the workforce, women's and children's right to the economic support of their husbands and fathers, women's exemption from military draft, and the right to privacy in bathrooms and dressing rooms. Removing these protections, church leaders believed, "would demean women rather than ennoble them."[15] They argued that nullifying these supposed benefits would also make the choice to embrace wife- and motherhood as a profession more difficult.

Third, the church feared the amendment would "encourag[e] those who promoted a unisex society," unmoored from gender norms and behaviors.[16] A unisex law, they warned, could facilitate such immoral behavior as homosexuality, abortion, and a "possible train" of unnamed "unnatural consequences" that could challenge "every morally accepted behavior pattern in America."[17] They were ambiguous about how exactly this parade of horribles might actually flow from women's constitutional equality, simply claiming that all manner of moral decadence would flow from the unisex society they believed the ERA would create. Fourth, the church claimed the ERA was a moral issue simply because the First Presidency defined it as such. A letter from the First Presidency in June 1979, to be read in church meetings the following Sunday, claimed that "only the First Presidency and the Twelve [Apostles] can declare a particular issue to be a moral issue worthy of full institutional involvement."[18]

The church's Gray Book also made legal claims about the ERA. It included a very alarmist and deceptively worded interpretation of the legislative history of the ERA as well as some court cases from states with state-level ERAs. It also claimed that the ERA would upset the balance of power between the states and the federal government and between the elected legislative branch and the appointed judicial branch of national government, concentrating power in the federal judiciary that was far better left to local officials.[19] The church stopped short of declaring its position against the ERA as a formal revelation (an issue I treat in chapter 3), but that it came in the form of three official letters from the First Presidency on church letterhead to all local leaders and read aloud in church meetings and later with the church magazine meant to most believers that it carried God's endorsement.

Few of the church's legal arguments were particularly unique to the LDS church and its representatives. Most had already been articulated by conservative congressional representatives and activists who opposed the ERA.[20] However, for Mormons, the moral threat took on an important theological valence because of the centrality of marriage and family to LDS theology about the meaning of life on earth and after death. For Mormons, a heterosexual "celestial" marriage covenant is required to enter the highest degree of heaven, where families "sealed" by priesthood power live together eternally. Heterosexual marriage is required of the faithful to live in God's presence after death, and family bonds are eternal. Thus, threats to marriage and family constituted moral threats not only on earth but in heaven as well, not only for this life but for the next.

Sonia's explanation for the church's ability to sway members' opinions and LDS women's activism against the ERA was not the moral or legal arguments the church made but quite simply church patriarchal authority. She claimed that the men of the church exercised such control over women simply because they could. They were God's patriarchal representatives on earth. Perhaps the most important reason for LDS women's activism, though, was articulated by Barbara Smith in a later interview. She said that the Relief Society "helped women understand that the work they were doing was vitally important."[21] LDS housewives and mothers found their roles as wives and mothers valued and encouraged by the church's position in ways that despite their best efforts, ERA proponents could not reproduce. D. Michael Quinn points out that "although LDS women were usually assigned to these activities by male priesthood leaders, for the most part these women enthusiastically participated in the anti-ERA campaign as an expression of their own deeply felt views."[22]

When the church called its members to actively work against the ERA in October 1978, thousands of church members, most of them women, became political activists overnight. In part under the direction of church leaders headquartered in Utah, local congregations mobilized armies of women into lobbying groups often called citizen's councils.[23] In these organizations, LDS women received instruction on how to lobby Congress. Women created and distributed anti-ERA materials for legislators and the general public, organized letter-writing campaigns (sometimes with supplied language), and boarded buses that were often arranged and paid for by priesthood leaders to attend anti-ERA rallies and legislative sessions to lobby.

In November 1978, church leaders in Sonia's area called a meeting to establish the organization that quickly became the VACC. Supporters of the ERA, though not Sonia herself, attended the meeting and compiled minutes from tape recordings and notes they took. For this reason, the minutes reflect the biases of these recorders. They are, however, the only extant record of the meeting. Here, I have emphasized elements of the meeting that Sonia highlighted in the months that followed as she quoted and mis-quoted the minutes of this meeting repeatedly in her public appearances.

The meeting began with Regional Representative Julian Lowe's introduc-tion, confirming that he and Regional Representative Don Ladd (who also served as chair of the LDS Washington, D.C. area Public Affairs Council) had decided to establish the organization "in the way the church has sug-gested" at the request of Gordon B. Hinckley.[24] Hinckley likely requested the creation of the organization in his capacity as head of the church's SAC, a committee the committee's secretary Richard Lindsay said was "mostly concerned with issues in the larger community and the environment in the church, in which the church functions."[25] Lowe then made his most con-troversial statement. The meeting minutes quote him as saying, "In other areas, we have found that it is not so good for the men to be so vociferous. It works against the *cause*. . . . If the brethren are out beating the bushes it looks like, in the eyes of some, that we are trying to keep the women subservient and it is far from that. This is the exact opposite of what we are trying to do, but it is always interpreted that way. Why don't I quit while I'm ahead."[26] Sonia made much of this statement in the months after this meeting.

The VACC was cochaired by Beverly Campbell and Jean Zundel. After Sonia's excommunication, Campbell came to play a central role at the national level as the church's official spokesperson on the ERA and eventually would become one of the best-known and influential conservative women authors of the twenty-first century.[27] At this meeting, though, Campbell took over following Lowe's initial remarks. She distributed a packet of information and declared that "this is the position of the Church. This is the position we would like you to take on this most important issue."[28] The contents of the packet and who put it together are unknown. The meeting proceeded with other speakers instructing the women on why they should oppose the ERA. At one point late in the meeting, a local church member who had been active in conservative Catholic activist Phyllis Schlafly's StopERA organization, Bob Beers, said, "If you go to your state senator and say that he should be against the Equal Rights Amendment because the Prophet . . . is against it, you are going to get nowhere. That may be why we are against it, but when you are trying to convince a legislator to do something he wants, you better talk his language, not yours."[29] That is, Beers suggested that the women needed to frame their opposition to the ERA in the political vocabularies of the legislators they were trying to convince, not in the religious terms that motivated their opposition to the ERA.

A bit later in the meeting, one audience member remarked that some LDS women supported the ERA and suggested that one's status in the church depended on opposing the ERA. Campbell responded, "That is not what we are saying. What is being said is women are being called because this is a moral issue. You are not being told that you have to be for or against the ERA. But indeed if this is your stand . . . if you feel that you follow the Prophet then we know where you stand. So there is no question."[30] Moments later, Campbell declared that "when the prophet speaks, he speaks scripture, right? He is the living voice of God on this earth. He has spoken." Some dissension and noise broke out as Campbell made this last statement.[31]

Opposing LDS Activism

The reports and minutes from MERA members who were present at this meeting, and similar reports from women in other states, shocked and dismayed Sonia. It looked to her like the church was directing and organizing its women's political activism from the leadership in Salt Lake City down through the church hierarchy to local priesthood leaders. Moreover, Sonia saw politics increasingly invading LDS church houses, meetings, homes, bank accounts, and minds. Sonia's problem was less that church authorities had taken a position than that they were actively organizing against the ERA behind the scenes, turning the church into a political organization.[32]

At first, Sonia was determined to oppose this anti-ERA activism through church-sanctioned channels. Shortly after the VACC organizing meeting, she and her MERA cofounders "went to [Lowe] and said 'since you have set up this organization, and it's a lobbying organization . . . what you have got ethically and morally to do is to send out a press release saying the Mormon Church [is] here and that we're a new lobbying organization, these are our beliefs . . . and we're going to go forth and do our work.'"[33] When Lowe refused to do any such thing, Sonia and her friends declared, "If you don't, we will."[34] Because Sonia was not working outside the home, she happened to be the one of the four women who had more flexible time. In an act she later said was "the beginning of the end of my membership" in the church, Sonia called a *Washington Post* reporter the next day.[35] "And I was terrified to do that. I was really a little Virginia housewife, my gosh, it scared the wits out of me, but I called up . . . the *Washington Post*. . . . It took two hours sitting by the phone to be able to pick it up! And I finally called in this little bitty voice, I said 'I don't suppose you'd be interested in knowing what the Mormons are doing against the ERA in Virginia?'" They were.[36] This was the beginning of Sonia's use of the press against the church's anti-ERA campaign, a strategy she used throughout both her campaign against LDS activism and her excommunication.

Sonia also thrice requested to meet with church president Spencer W. Kimball. Her intent was to discuss the pain that the church's position was causing pro-ERA women and invite him to reconsider. She believed that if she could speak with Kimball, she could convince him to change the church's stance. She was rebuffed. In Sonia's mind, Kimball's refusal to meet with her and other pro-ERA women demonstrated church leaders' unwillingness to listen to women and the futility of objecting to the church's politics through official channels. This impelled Sonia to use the press with even more fervor to publicize the church's role in politics and to hold accountable church leaders whose doors and ears were closed to women.

Over the late 1970s and early 1980s, the church and its members mobilized campaigns against the ERA in several states (most notably in Arizona, California, Florida, Georgia, Illinois, Missouri, Montana, Nevada, South

Carolina, Virginia, and Washington). Women around the country reported that the ERA was condemned from the LDS pulpit, anti-ERA petitions circulated in meetinghouse lobbies, young men's priesthood organizations distributed pamphlets, and letter-writing meetings were held at meetinghouses and homes. Members were instructed to go home from church with plans to call their congressional representatives to vote against the ERA. For Sonia, this indicated that church leaders determined the meaning and significance of the ERA so the men of the church, not the women the ERA would directly affect, interpreted how the amendment would affect women's, gender, and family issues. The men then deployed this analysis to mobilize the women against their own interests. Because Sonia believed that local priesthood leaders took their direction from the church's Special Affairs Committee, headed by Gordon B. Hinckley, she made little distinction between the leadership of local bishops, stake presidents, and regional representatives and the leadership of church authorities in Salt Lake City. For her, LDS men's participation in a rigidly structured, tightly organized and deeply obedient priesthood hierarchy meant lockstep agreement with and execution of the demands of the First Presidency. For this reason, she often referred interchangeably to church leaders in Salt Lake, all priesthood holders collectively, or any cluster of individual priesthood holders as "the men of the church" or, more simply and more frequently, just "the men." Sonia believed that it was the men's religious authority over women that facilitated their hermeneutic and political power to convince women to follow the men's lead.

At least until late 1979, Sonia hoped that her activism would save the church from itself. Because the men would not listen to her, she turned to the media. As she explained to a friend, "How is the Prophet going to understand that he needs to ask for revelation if he doesn't know there is a problem? . . . So we thought we would help in that process." MERA founders knew the church cared about its public image, particularly as a proselytizing church. So according to Sonia,

> We thought to ourselves, what does the church listen to, what is important to it? It values media. [The] church is a very large media-conscious group, alright, let us get this through the media, then they cannot help but notice us, so that's why we began flying our banners. You know, we did it, to begin with, out of love for the church. I know that's impossible for people to believe. We really wanted the church to begin to see the problem, begin to do something about it before the whole thing blew up.[37]

It is important to emphasize that although she critiqued it powerfully, Sonia also deeply loved the church before her excommunication. She told pro-ERA LDS women to remain active members: "We can't leave it like rats from a sinking ship." The church "doesn't belong to those men. It belongs to us too and we have an obligation to stay in."[38] She saw herself as keeping the church honest and accountable and encouraging course correction when she saw the men straying from the church's spiritual mission into clandestine and dishonest political activity. However, the church found Sonia, rather than itself, in need of saving.

Sonia's opposition to the church's veiled political tactics primarily took the form of making them public. She could never have anticipated the level of national attention she received, but in the wake of her 1978 fiery exchange with Utah senator Orrin Hatch, Sonia came to understand the power of the press and was eager to exploit it on behalf of the ERA. As the public face of MERA, she actively sought media attention to expose the anti-ERA activity the men of the church were directing.[39] "The main reason we do things is that we want to get into the press time and time again. . . . We are insisting on dragging the church and its Equal Rights Amendment stand through the media every single time we can, not to let them off the hook."[40] Sonia strategized to maximize press coverage, and she was very skilled at it. Her amusing and sometimes confrontational tactics often got front-page attention, especially in Utah, Virginia, and nearby Washington, D.C. Sonia believed her success at courting press attention was a central factor in her excommunication. As she likely knew from growing up in an LDS community, "it's a real taboo in the church to make public any controversy."[41] In part because of her skill with the press, most media initially focused their coverage of both the church's early LDS anti-ERA campaigns and Sonia's excommunication from Sonia's point of view. Also, until early 1980, church leaders refused to talk to reporters, so early press coverage largely featured Sonia's perspective.

The Excommunication

Sonia had the sense in March 1979 that her bishop, Jeffrey Willis, "was looking pretty hard for something. And he told me that he was thinking of holding a[n excommunication] court and I said 'oh, you mustn't do it.'" Willis responded, in Sonia's words, that "'it seems to me that it's going to be necessary.'"[42] Sonia was and remains completely convinced that her excommunication was centrally directed from church headquarters in Salt Lake City. She believes high-level church leaders hounded Willis, almost daily toward the end of 1979, to excommunicate her. Apparently, Willis refused to do some of the things leaders in Salt Lake City asked him to and resisted excommunicating Sonia for several months.[43]

Sonia has always maintained that she was excommunicated because of her politics, not for any doctrinal or moral offense. As the threat of excommunication heated up, Sonia told one reporter, "They know they can't try me for freedom of speech or political action. So they have to trump up some charge, to do a little witch hunt."[44] As her excommunication loomed, however, Sonia became increasingly dismayed that press coverage was more interested in the "family feud" between a lone woman and a powerful church than in the politics of the church's anti-ERA activity. As Linda Sillitoe observed, "The press was much more interested in the personal angle of a toeing-all-lines-but-one Mormon woman battling her (male) church leaders on an issue of women's rights. That angle made good copy and the story of the Church's politics was mainly ignored, except as it was embodied in one quotable personality—Sonia Johnson."[45] Sonia explained that her personal drama made for more interesting copy, but her criticisms of the secrecy of the church's campaign suggest she also believed, perhaps correctly, that most people did not know the church or its members were so politically engaged against the ERA.[46] Sonia was more able to draw public attention to the church's anti-ERA activities with in-person speeches at political meetings and rallies, which rarely made the news but mobilized feminist activists. Over the course of 1978 and 1979, press coverage of Sonia's activism waxed and waned, but it exploded on November 14, 1979, when Willis's counselors (assistants to the bishop) hand delivered to Sonia's home a letter requesting her presence at a bishop's court three days later. The letter contained no charges.[47] Sheldon Rampton, a student at Princeton who was at Sonia's home when the summons to a church court was delivered, leaked the news to the press.[48]

Given the amount of press coverage her situation was attracting, Sonia warned her church leaders that excommunication would be a bad public relations move. "I said, if you want to get the ERA ratified, you just have to begin doing things like this."[49] Nonetheless, church leaders moved forward with Sonia's excommunication. The letter had given her only three days to prepare for the trial. Initially, Willis agreed to postpone the trial another ten days. Minutes later, Sonia called Stake President Earl Roueche, Willis's ecclesiastical superior, and asked him to take over the trial. She told Roueche, "I know that he [Willis] is going to bungle this matter."[50] Later the same evening, however, Willis told Sonia that by Roueche's authority, the trial would indeed occur on November 17 as scheduled. Sonia stayed up all night writing a formal "Request for Extension of Time."

When Sonia arrived at the church for her trial (a five-hour meeting that turned out to be more of a "pretrial hearing," so-called after the fact), about one hundred supporters, and thirty or forty reporters had gathered at the church house.[51] Before Sonia entered the trial, Michael Barrett, an attorney friend of hers who had offered advice, had arranged with Willis that Sonia could record the trial if she agreed never to request her own copy of the recording. Weeks before the pretrial meeting, Roueche had also told Sonia she would be able to record any trial proceedings that occurred.[52] However, after the opening prayer, Sonia asked several times to tape record the trial to keep a record of it and was repeatedly refused.[53] Sonia then asked for another person to witness the trial for her protection, a request also denied. Sonia ultimately convinced Willis to allow her more time to prepare her defense by asking, "Would Jesus Christ deny me some extra time?"[54] Willis postponed the trial until December 1 to allow Sonia more time to prepare her defense. Sonia reports that she spent the rest of the meeting "organizing" her accusers to come up with formal charges. Sonia and her accusers agreed on a set of charges and to continue the trial two weeks later, on December 1. She was still not given a written record of those charges, but she believed she could successfully defend herself against them.

As Sonia got up to leave the meeting, her church leaders told her she must not discuss the proceedings with the press. Leaders felt that the trial was sacred and private. But Sonia felt that her trial was public and political, and especially in the absence of a recording or a witness, she felt she had to mobilize the press to keep church leaders honest and accountable.[55] She viewed this publicity as only fair play since the church was using its religious authority to try to silence her political voice. At the end of her pretrial hearing, one leader in the meeting accused her of "just doing this to get publicity." Sonia replied, "I am not doing this at all, you are. I didn't want this trial. But as long as you have done it, and the press is there, I will use it. And I want you to know that I will use it for the ERA as long as it's available,"[56] which she did. However, she also told her accusers, "If you deal honorably with me, I will tell them [the press] so. If you do not deal with me honorably, I will tell them so. It's entirely up to you."[57]

The next day, Willis visited Sonia's home, and Sonia was struck by Willis's "almost total incoherence, his air of being about to fall apart. He was a man caught in a true dilemma, being pulled fiercely in two directions at once."[58] Sonia believed Willis did not want to excommunicate her but was being compelled by church leaders in Salt Lake City. At one point between the pretrial meeting and the trial, Willis seems to have threatened "to have a quiet private little kangaroo court" without notice or witnesses unless Sonia stopped talking to the press.[59] Sonia believed that the presence and integrity of attorney Michael Barrett, an LDS attorney and friend who advised Sonia during her trial, saved her from this fate. Willis moved forward with the December 1 date.

A few days before her December 1 trial, a letter from Willis informed Sonia that "your 'cause' is not on trial and remind you that your witnesses will be permitted to address only the issues of the court."[60] This would come to mean that witnesses and Sonia herself were forbidden to discuss or *even mention* the ERA. At this point, Sonia still had no written record of the charges against her, only the verbal agreement she and her accusers had reached during her pretrial hearing. Between her pretrial hearing and her trial, Sonia gathered eight witnesses, some of whom flew to Virginia from far away. When she arrived at the church the evening of her trial, a few hundred people had gathered outside the church building in the bitter cold, with many reporters and photographers in the crowd. This time, Sonia said, she knew from the moment the trial began that her fate was already decided. Willis read several charges not agreed to in the pretrial hearing, many of which Sonia had never heard before.[61] Five people plus Sonia herself testified, but by the time they finished, Sonia felt that the rest of her witnesses would be useless and that her case had already been decided.[62] She called no more witnesses. Sonia later poignantly regretted that her mother had not had the chance to testify on her behalf.[63] After some discussion, Sonia left the room and headed for reporters waiting outside, again harnessing the power of the press in her struggle against church leaders.

Meanwhile, reporters had been documenting the vigil outside the church house. After Sonia emerged, she reiterated to one reporter her sense that her offenses were political, not religious. She said that the statements that were at issue in the trial "would have been inconsequential . . . if I hadn't been doing ERA." She said, "My political activity has been aimed against theirs, it's angered them. That's the real offense. But they can't try me for that."[64] When asked about the delay in the outcome, she said of her judges, "I really think they mean to be kind and have time to make a difficult decision."[65] Minutes later, Willis emerged and read a statement saying simply that a trial had been conducted in accordance with church doctrine in which Sonia's position on the ERA was not an issue. He said that a decision had not yet been made but would be forthcoming. He also clarified that Sonia's trial was not related to any moral or sexual impropriety, apparently quashing rumors to the contrary.[66]

The charges at issue in Sonia's December 1 trial appear in the written historical record only in retrospect. On December 5, four days after her trial, Sonia received Willis's letter informing her that she had been excommunicated. It read, in part, "As you know, I have at no time tried to dissuade you from seeking ratification of the [Equal Rights] Amendment. I have counseled with you relative to your support of Church leaders and doctrine." He continued that her public comments about church leaders and doctrines prompted her trial. She was found guilty of three formal charges and one informal charge. The formal charges are as follows:

> You testified that you believe and have taught that (Mormon) missionaries should not be invited into people's homes.
> You believe and have publicly stated that our society, specifically including Church leaders has "a savage misogyny" when in fact it is church doctrine that exaltation can be gained only through the love that results in the eternal bonding of man and woman.
> You have publicly taught that the church is dedicated to imposing the prophet's moral directives upon all Americans when it is the doctrine of the church that all people are free to choose for themselves those moral directives dictated by their own consciences.

The informal charge, not listed in the letter as a "charge" but rather simply a sentence, was that

> your testimony and public speeches evidence in spirit that you are not in harmony with church doctrine concerning the nature of God and the manner in which He directs His church on earth.[67]

Willis's letter to Sonia excommunicating her also formed the basis for a press conference in Salt Lake City in which Don LeFevre from the public relations office of the church read the letter and answered questions. He reiterated that support of the ERA was not at issue and that "a person's support of ERA or any other public issue like that is certainly not grounds for a court action in the church."[68]

The first charge Willis listed was rooted in a statement Sonia made in Kalispell, Montana in August 1979. The LDS church had been campaigning vigorously against the ERA in Montana, and the Montana chapter of NOW had invited Sonia to help them deal with their "Mormon problem." Sonia had been told that Montana NOW members were already refusing to speak to LDS missionaries because of the church's position on the ERA.[69] In the Montana speech, Sonia pointed out that Mormons were a very proselytizing people, and "we've got a good thing going and we'd like you to hear about it." She told attendees that the church was very concerned about its public image, so "those who are directing this ERA activity need a taste of the consequences of their behavior, and one of the things everybody can do is write them and call them, the very headquarters of the church, and say you are outraged that the Mormons are working against equal civil rights for women, that if their missionaries ever come to your doors, you wouldn't consider letting them in."[70] Sonia's intended message was that refusing to speak with missionaries because the church opposed the ERA would do little good unless church leaders actually knew about it.

To some, the distinction between instructing listeners not to let missionaries in and telling listeners who were already refusing to speak with missionaries to tell church leaders why they were doing so may be a fine one, but to Sonia, it was significant. For her, the statement was simple political lobbying. The church had chosen to enter the political arena and so could be fought politically. She was "saying, 'if you will listen to me, I'll listen to you. I'll gladly listen to your missionaries if you'll unhand my equal rights.'"[71] More significant, however, was that Sonia's Kalispell remark was misquoted widely in the press. Diane Weathers reported in *Newsweek*, for example, that Sonia had said, "If a missionary comes to your door, tell him you are not interested in a church that is fighting equal rights."[72] Sonia produced a recording of the speech at her December 1 trial. Regardless, church leaders were unable or unwilling to accept, or it did not matter to them, that Sonia had been speaking to an audience already refusing to speak to missionaries or that Sonia had been misquoted in the press. To them, Sonia had assaulted and endangered the church's missionary program.

The second charge leveraged against Sonia was rooted in a paper she gave at the Utah Women's Conference in October 1979, titled "Off Our Pedestals, or the Chronicles of the Uppity Sisters." Sonia's remarks were again misquoted in the press by Linda Thielke, a part-time reporter for United Press International. Thielke quoted and then misinterpreted the scope of Sonia's savage misogyny statement. Thielke wrote, "'Pedestals are the pits,' said Ms. Johnson. It shows most vividly the savage misogeny [sic] in the Mormon church."[73] Sonia, however, said nothing in this statement about the church itself. Rather, she had claimed that "the pedestal as a symbol of women's immobilization and isolation in our male-centered society, more than any other symbol . . . reveals our savage misogyny."[74] The context was clear that by "our male centered society" Sonia meant neither Mormons nor the church specifically but all of Western society. The rest of the speech detailed a developing Mormon feminist consciousness, showing instances of LDS women "finding the courage to clambor [sic] up off their pedestals and to face their full humanity."[75] The point of the speech was to provide an example of women resisting misogyny everywhere, not just in the LDS church.

When Sonia brought this to the attention of her accusers, they responded by asking whether Sonia would include church leaders in the category of people possessing a "savage misogyny." She answered that "I thought they were not immune to such influences."[76] The point of the speech was that no one was immune to the influence of patriarchy—not even the women the speech celebrated or even Sonia herself. Unable or unwilling to understand the nuances of Sonia's argument, church leaders pressed Sonia repeatedly to admit that she believed church leaders to be misogynists. She finally admitted begrudgingly, "yes." Willis found Sonia guilty of the second charge.

The source for the third charge Willis's letter outlined, that Sonia accused the church of imposing the prophet's moral directives on all Americans, is most likely from a speech Sonia gave at the national American Psychological Association (APA) conference in New York City in September 1979. This speech, titled "Patriarchal Panic: Sexual Politics in the Mormon Church" was surely Sonia's most intemperate. In it, she called the church "the last unmitigated Western patriarchy" and accused Mormons of believing that "when our leaders speak, the thinking has been done."[77] For Sonia, the implications of this "mass renunciation of individual conscience" was that "the Mormons, a tiny minority, are dedicated to imposing the Prophet's moral directives upon all Americans." The men of the church, she claimed, had "put women under total male control" and "have seriously harmed women's self-esteem, lowered our status, made us bootlickers and toadies to the men of the Church and destroyed what little freedom of choice we had."[78] The implication was that the women of the church did their men's anti-ERA bidding not out of authentic choice but because they were controlled by the men.

Sonia's speech also accused church leaders of fearing the equality the ERA would give women. She quoted Kimball's interview with the Associated Press in which Kimball warned pro-ERA women to be "'very, very careful' because the church is led by 'strong men and able men. . . . We feel we are in a position to lead them properly.'" The meaning of Kimball's statement, Sonia said, was that women "had better be very, very careful because the men at the head of the Church are strong and the patriarchs have for millennia crushed those women who escaped from their mind-bendings."[79] The upshot was that the LDS campaign against the ERA reflected male leaders' "raw panic at the idea that women might step forward as goddesses-in-the-making with power in a real . . . sense."[80] Sonia celebrated that in Mormon women's feminist awakening and in the women's movement more generally "can be heard—distinctly—the death rattle of the patriarchy."[81] Sonia's APA speech was likely her only that used this kind of vitriol and comprised this kind of attack on church policies and leaders. The day of her excommunication, Sonia admitted she had "used some stronger rhetoric than was necessary" in the speech and had "offered to repent for that language."[82]

Sonia's response to the more general charge that the prophet was imposing his moral directives on the entire nation was that it was simply true. She "challenge[d] anyone to demonstrate that I have lied" and claimed she should not be excommunicated for telling the truth.[83] If the church did not want her to describe its behavior, she contended, "they should stop doing it. Because it certainly isn't evil to tell what is actually happening; it's not evil to tell the truth."[84]

It is difficult to know what to make of Willis's fourth informal charge, that Sonia's "testimony and public speeches" were "not in harmony with church doctrine concerning the nature of God and the manner in which He directs His church on earth." Sonia's statements against the ERA never occurred in a context in which she could reasonably be thought to be preaching or exercising any religious authority. However, as I examine more thoroughly in chapter 3, among Mormons, distinctions between religion and politics are much more permeable than in most other Christian faiths, and Sonia did publicly criticize church leaders.

Moreover, as Sonia pointed out, whatever distinction the church made between religion and politics was made by its male leaders. For her, these territorial disputes were shot through with gender because those Sonia believed were exercising religious authority in political arenas were men, while those losing their political freedom as a result were women. Both Sonia and the church and its representatives deployed distinctions between religion and politics, between church and state, in ways that served their ends. For Sonia, these questions about revelation and policy, religion and politics, had political implications but not religious or doctrinal ones. For the church, however, Sonia's critiques had doctrinal and religious implications alongside political ones.

In this context, it was important to Sonia that all but one of the criticisms at issue in the trial, the APA speech, occurred in the context of ERA politics, not religion. Immediately after her trial, she said, "Everything I've said that is alarming to them I've said in ERA speeches—well, almost everything."[85] For this reason, Sonia felt that the ERA was central to the excommunication proceedings because it was necessary that her accusers understand her dismay at the church's secretive anti-ERA activism, the context in which Sonia made the offending statements, and her motivations for making them. "If you can't understand how I feel about the Equal Rights Amendment and how I feel about the church's being in politics, how can you understand what I'm saying in a speech?"[86] However, by Sonia's account, her accusers forbade any discussion of the ERA so they could maintain the facade that the ERA was not at issue in the trial. For Sonia, the effect of this ban was to intimidate and silence her witnesses, most of whom had come with statements written without knowledge of or warning about the ban: "Everybody who was trying to talk about those speeches had to keep . . . saying 'ERA,' and when they did, [church leaders would] say, 'that's out of order,' or 'we're not going to talk about the ERA.'"[87] So distressing was this to Sonia that she did not even call some of her witnesses because she knew their testimony would mention the ERA, so they simply "wouldn't get anywhere."[88] Nonetheless, Willis's excommunication letter to Sonia told her that "your witnesses were heard and your evidence presented to your acknowledged satisfaction."[89] She remarked in her memoir that "neither my witnesses nor my evidence was heard to my satisfaction. . . . I decided against calling the other witnesses because the court was refusing to hear testimony, not because I felt all had been satisfactorily heard."[90]

From when Sonia was informed of a trial until her last appeal was exhausted (excepting a few brief moments), Sonia publicly demonstrated a perhaps naive conviction that her excommunication was not a foregone conclusion from the time it began.[91] When reporters asked church spokesperson LeFevre if Sonia's excommunication was "initiated from Church headquarters," he responded, "Absolutely not. That would be improper. The Church procedure would call for this to be handled entirely on a local basis." LeFevre then stated, twice, that he did not know whether Willis had been in contact with church authorities in Salt Lake City or if they were involved in the decision.[92] The church's position that Willis excommunicated Sonia of his own accord was widely reported in the press and the church has since continued to take that stance.

On January 2, 1980, in a church press release from the director of press relations for the church public communication office, Jerry P. Cahill again clarified the church's position that Sonia was not excommunicated for her support of the ERA. "But, in her advocacy of ERA, Mrs. Johnson expressed attitudes and views which went beyond that issue and constituted a direct and irresponsible attack upon the church, its leaders, doctrines and programs." In addition to the charges in Willis's letter, Sonia had "misrepresented and held up to ridicule the leadership and membership of the church."[93]

Twelve days after her excommunication, Sonia appealed Willis's decision to his ecclesiastical superior (the same man who had initially denied her extra time), Stake President Roueche, claiming the trial was "based on erroneous information" and was "procedurally flawed."[94] The statement detailed her responses to the charges, claiming the statements informing the three charges were misquoted, taken out of context, or simply true of the church. Sonia also pointed to a number of procedural errors and injustices she had endured over the course of her trial. Sonia also claimed publicly that Willis's reasons and the church's explanations were pretexts for what really irked the men of the church. Her "unforgivable offense was that I went to unratified states and told what Mormons were doing in those states. . . . I was opposing their political campaign. . . . That's why they excommunicated me, because I was having some political power."[95] She continued her political activity unabated.

It took Roueche more than two months to deny Sonia's appeal. He read his decision to Sonia on the front steps of her home, but Sonia was not allowed to keep a copy. Roueche flat-out denied any procedural misconduct and pointed out that "your conduct has been observed to ascertain if there was an attitudinal change concerning the church leadership, its position on moral issues, or if there were expressions of any such change. I regret that I have not found any such change."[96] The excommunication would stand. He acknowledged that Sonia could appeal the decision to President Kimball.

A few weeks after Roueche rejected her appeal, Sonia sent church president Kimball an extensive letter asking the First Presidency to retry her case, along with a copy of her previous appeal to Roueche. She wrote primarily to "personally plead with you to vindicate my rights and the rights of other members to take a political position at variance with that of the Church without fear of either formal or informal religious repression."[97] The First Presidency refused to retry the case, saying instead that it would reach a decision to uphold or reverse Sonia's excommunication based on the existing trial record and supporting documents. Sonia wrote Kimball a second time requesting a retrial, telling him, "You have stood as an ensign of courage and justice, I hope you do so again."[98] Sonia's appeal was again denied, this time via a letter from Kimball's secretary, Francis M. Gibbons. A short time later, Sonia told a reporter that the entire process of excommunication and appeal "makes me heartsick. It is so dishonorable."[99]

Disciplining Feminism

Sonia reported repeatedly and in public that her trial was an example of the unjust ways the men of the church mistreated women when it came to the ERA. Willis had initially told Sonia she would receive more time to prepare her defense—Roueche overruled that decision. Sonia had asked to receive written charges to prepare her defense—she did not. She was told she could tape record the trial—she could not. Her witnesses were intimidated. Willis's excommunication letter put words in her mouth that she did not say, that her witnesses had been heard to her satisfaction—they had not. She asked repeatedly to receive some record of her trial in order to prepare her appeals—she did not. She saw the multiple ways she felt dismissed and deceived and her trust breached by the church officials who tried her as representative of how the men of the church dismissed women's issues and how they deceived and breached the trust of the women who followed their lead.

In another sense, though, Sonia's excommunication was an individual instance of larger issues about the hermeneutical, religious, and political authority Sonia believed LDS men exercised to contain the feminist ideas and activism of church members. If Sonia could not use the press to stop the men from excommunicating her, she could at least use it to keep them honest and, failing that, to expose their dishonorable behavior both in relationship to her and in their manipulation of other LDS women to do their political bidding. For Sonia, these two exposures were intimately related. She came to view her excommunication as an attempt by church leaders to bring not only her but other pro-ERA LDS women (and supportive men) to heel and was as determined to expose this tactic as she was to exposing the church's anti-ERA activism.[100]

Once the threat that Sonia might be excommunicated became widely known, the church maintained that supporting the ERA would not be grounds for excommunication. However, it is impossible to know how much of the church's stance was an effect of the negative attention Sonia's excommunication had focused on the church. In one of Sonia's most public statements, when asked if other pro-ERA LDS women might be excommunicated, Sonia told the audience of *Donahue*, a popular nationally syndicated talk show, that "there is real danger. . . . It's beginning to look like it could be a blood bath."[101] She also reported that women had told her they had been excommunicated for working with a women's shelter, working in or helping start a battered women's shelter, or simply vocally supporting the ERA.[102] Other observers agreed with Sonia's analysis. Mark Leone, the head of anthropology at the University of Maryland, College Park agreed. He told the *Washington Star* that Sonia's primary offense was "talking to other Mormons." Church discipline existed "to form community consensus" and show other Mormons "the things the hierarchy believes are improper behavior."[103] A few weeks later, *Washington Herald* reporter Vera Glaser reported that "interviews with dozens of excommunicants, members attempting to withdraw and members in good standing reveal that the Church, through its leaders in the wards (neighborhood churches), had been quietly excommunicating ERA advocates for months before the Sonia case drew national attention." At the same time, Marilee Latta, president of Utah Equal Rights Coalition told Glaser that "anyone who says there are no pressures on ERA supporters is not speaking the truth. . . . The pressures are tremendous."[104]

Some LDS women experienced vague, primarily low-level threats from fellow church members while others faced threats of formal church discipline from local leaders. It is unknown how many of these were carried out. One form of social censure was questioning the faithfulness of pro-ERA Mormons.[105] Members told Glaser of harassment and intimidation from their church leaders, while others "say they are afraid to speak out because of possible reprisals in the tightly knit Mormon community." A woman under a pseudonym reported to Glaser that she had been shunned for her bumper sticker that read, "Another Mormon for ERA": "They canceled me from their Christian family as surely and as certainly as if they had physically killed me." Others faced threats and sometimes low-level forms of formal church discipline. Joyce Slechta of Mission Viejo, California belonged to MERA but was told that "if I did anything too actively to promote it I would be reprimanded. At the same time they kept saying you can freely do what you want." Glaser interviewed women who reported being removed from church callings, or feared their husbands would lose jobs with the church or lost their temple recommends (a pass that allows Mormons in good standing to enter LDS temples to perform rituals). One member said that the ERA "is not the reason our bishops gave. They pin it on something vague like preaching false doctrine." If these accounts are accurate, this suggests that Sonia's public excommunication was more a crescendo of church discipline than either a beginning or an end. As historian Colleen McDannell suggests, "suspicion, judgment, condemnation and fear colored the post-ERA period."[106] Church representatives denied these accounts, however. Jerry Cahill told Glaser that he did not know "of a single other excommunication," claiming that Sonia "really knows how to milk it, doesn't she?"[107] (It is important to note here that because most excommunications are conducted and decided by local authorities, they could very easily have existed without Cahill knowing about them.)

Whether church leaders intended it or not, the historical record is clear that both the informal threat of social censure and the formal threat of church discipline intimidated and silenced many pro-ERA LDS women. Kathleen Flake, for example, reported in the wake of Sonia's ordeal, "Fully terrorized by the raw power of the Church in political matters, I, like so many of my sisters, hit the deck. . . . I just faded away into law school and benign inactivity in the Church."[108] Church power contained the forms LDS feminism and activism could take and limited the number and nature of Mormons who publicly supported the ERA. Many members remained quite frightened even after church leaders declared supporting the ERA would not be grounds for church discipline. Sonia's excommunication reinforced those fears regardless of how fervently church leaders tried to get ahead of them. Mormon Women's Forum founder Kelli Frame may have been correct in asserting in 1990 that "Sonia Johnson was excommunicated so the rest of us would not be."[109]

These disciplinary effects affected members' positions on the ERA. One reporter said that when NOW's "ERA missionaries" canvassed in Utah in the summer of 1981, many church members would sign a pro-ERA petition addressed to U.S. president Ronald Reagan, but far fewer were willing to sign one addressed to church president Kimball. They feared signing the letter because they depended on the church for their salvation, and they feared the social censure that might result if neighbors saw their names.[110] In 1982, John Unger Zussman and Shauna M. Adix reported that almost 70 percent of Mormons polled supported the text of the ERA when identified as "an amendment which is currently being considered by the legislature" and not as the Equal Rights Amendment. When identified by name and not by text, however, that number dropped to just under 33 percent. Of those who said they opposed the ERA by name, a majority supported the text of the ERA when not labeled as such. Only 3 percent of respondents recognized the text *as* the amendment. Zussman and Adix conjectured that "the church's strong anti-ERA position has shaped the views of citizens and legislators" while respondents showed significant ignorance and misconceptions of the amendment.[111] In the words of D. Michael Quinn, "The Mormon hierarchy's official rejection was apparently what made the difference" between supporting the text of the ERA and opposing the ERA by name.[112]

46

As Sonia pointed out, many of the issues swirling around her excommunication and its aftermath were small-scale iterations of larger issues in the church's campaigns against the ERA. The distinction Sonia made between religion and politics during her trial was central to her public activism against the church and was widely discussed in the national press and among church members. Sonia claimed, simply, that the church, a religious organization, was sticking its nose where it did not belong, in the nation's political affairs. Moreover, Sonia believed it was doing so secretly and deceptively, hiding behind the activism of women members while asking them to lie. For Sonia, the injustice of her excommunication, alongside male leaders' unwillingness to listen to her or her witnesses, paralleled their unwillingness to listen to women at all, while still exploiting their religious sentiments toward the church's political ends. The next two chapters turn to these larger issues.

CHAPTER THREE

"A Compromise with Integrity that It Simply Cannot Afford"

The Gendered Ethics of Revelation, Religion, and Politics

Less than three weeks after her excommunication, Sonia declared on the front page of the Metro section of the *Washington Post*, "I'm concerned that the Church's covert and less-than-strictly-ethical political activities may be a compromise with integrity that it simply cannot afford. Even institutions reap what they sow."[1] This statement referenced both the church's anti-ERA activities and her excommunication, which she viewed in large part as exemplary of larger problems of gender, power, and ethics in the church. For her, the ways she was dishonorably treated during her excommunication paralleled the ways the men of the church treated women, and she believed the institution would come to pay for both.

This chapter examines two sets of related issues that framed Sonia's concerns. First, Sonia's critiques of the church's anti-ERA activism rested on the conviction that its anti-ERA position was policy, not revelation. The crucial difference between policy and revelation in the church is that policy merely relates to the earthly management of God's church by imperfect humans, while revelation is understood to be the direct unmitigated word of God. Second, because Sonia believed the church's opposition to the ERA was policy, not revelation, she found it a secular political stance, not a religious one. Thus, she believed she could oppose the church politically without compromising her religious convictions. These two sets of issues, policy versus revelation and politics versus religion, collapsed on each other to raise difficult questions about the nature of continuing revelation, the role of the president of the church, and the nature and extent of religious authority. Thus, Sonia's critiques challenged prophetic and priesthood authority in nuanced gendered ways. As Sonia publicly pointed out, continuing revelation on behalf of all or parts of the church community was primarily a male entitlement. So were policy decisions. In the context of the ERA, Sonia breathed renewed life into gendered questions around the scope of religious authority, who in the church had what kind of authority over what, and who decided.

The ERA: Policy or Revelation?

An important doctrinal innovation of Mormonism that distinguishes it from most other forms of Christianity is the theological principle of continuing revelation. Joseph Smith, founder of the faith, wrote in one of the church's articles of faith that "we believe all that God has revealed, all that He does now reveal, and we believe that He will yet reveal many great and important things pertaining to the Kingdom of God."[2] Smith established that God would continue to reveal His will to future prophets. The doctrine of continuing revelation has had varied implications across LDS history. In the early years of the church, prophets Joseph Smith and Brigham Young exercised considerable revelatory power over church matters and often over the daily affairs of members.

Riding shotgun with the doctrine of continuing revelation was early Mormonism's entangling of spiritual and temporal affairs together under the banner of religion. As scholars J. Spencer Fluhman, Benjamin E. Park, Kathleen Flake, and I have each demonstrated in different ways, these questions about what "counts" as religion and what does not are nearly as old as the church itself.[3] The early church made little distinction between spiritual and temporal affairs or between religion and politics. Religion crept into many elements of church members' lives in ways that many Americans found disturbing. Several anti-Mormons observed that the faith's unique mixing of the sacred and the profane pushed it "out of the sphere of religion."[4] Over the late nineteenth and early twentieth centuries, the church rather deliberately "Americanized" its cultural, political, and marital practices, adopting a much more limited Protestant view of religion as a matter of private belief that had little political, temporal, or public relevance, finally subordinating church to state, prophecy to democracy.[5]

By the 1970s, church leaders became concerned that the church was losing its distinctiveness among Christian faiths. One response was "renewed efforts by the presiding authorities to reassert the charismatic and prophetic element" of Mormonism.[6] In this context, church opposition to the ERA was "not so much an expression of sheer patriarchal obstinacy as it [was] yet another assertion of the integrity and charisma of the prophetic office in the face of pressure for political expediency."[7] The role of the president of the church in relationship to this doctrine was changing during the latter half of the twentieth century from considering the church president primarily as an administrative leader to thinking of him as primarily a prophet in frequent communication with God, "strengthening the president's role as God's mouthpiece on earth." This shift culminated during Spencer W. Kimball's presidency, which lasted from 1975 to 1983, giving Kimball new influence over the beliefs, choices, and lives of church members.[8] Hence, church members were likely more inclined to think of the church's ERA position as revealed or inspired than previously.

For LDS women activists on all sides, few questions were as central as whether the church's position against the ERA was revelation. More broadly, Sonia's critiques of church leaders spoke to critical issues of theology, authority, and belief that touched nerves on many levels of the church and on all sides of the debate. Some ERA supporters lost faith in church leaders. Others believed Sonia's critiques went too far. At the same time, some ERA opponents were enraged by Sonia's critiques, while others (though fewer) empathized with her position. All Mormons interested in the ERA, and probably many who were not, had to reckon in some way with the challenges Sonia posed to the church and male priesthood authority.

Sonia's uncertainty around the revelatory status of the church's anti-ERA position initially presented her with a serious dilemma. She was painfully unsatisfied that the church left ambiguous the status and stakes of its opposition to the ERA. For her, if the church's opposition to the ERA was a revelation, God himself was a sexist who opposed women's rights. If it was not a revelation, then the women of the church were not important enough to Kimball to merit a revelation. Only after a "terrific conflict" did Sonia conclude that the church's opposition to the ERA was not a revelation but a policy, so she could oppose the church's position in good faith.[9]

Especially before her excommunication and after she had exhausted church-sanctioned channels of inquiry, one way Sonia garnered press attention was by publicly demanding that the prophet actually state whether he had received a revelation regarding the ERA. She said on one newscast that "we are urging through every channel we know for church leaders to make this clear."[10] Because women were half the population of the world and at least half of the membership of the church, Sonia believed that the ERA "is worthy of revelation. If [the Prophet has] had a revelation, I deserve to know it. If he hasn't, he should ask for one because we [women] are worth it."[11] Sentences like these publicly insulted Kimball's dedication to women members of the church, challenging him to advocate with God on their behalf. At the same time, Sonia told the press that church leaders' claims to knowledge of and authority over LDS women's needs and women's lives was devastatingly uninformed because they refused to listen to the women they claimed to lead. For example, she pointed out the "problematic arrogance" of male church leaders in publishing a book about women with essays by fifteen male church authorities but not a single woman.[12]

In beseeching Kimball to either declare or receive a revelation about the ERA and in insulting his understanding of women in the church, Sonia publicly challenged his prophetic authority in a time when it was perhaps at its apex. Especially because, as a woman, Sonia had no role in the priesthood hierarchy, many members saw her behavior as overstepping her boundaries with her demand that the prophet bow to her requests. At the same time, Sonia pointed out that the prophet was exploiting the unclarity of the church's position, accusing Kimball of withholding clarity about the revelatory status of his opposition to the ERA in the interest of manipulating members' political sentiments. He was "acting like it's a revelation, therefore it's a revelation, and he's never had to say." Thus, Kimball and the priesthood hierarchy he headed allowed women to believe that their anti-ERA activism was God's will. For Sonia, "if [Kimball] should say what he must say, in the end, which I believe is that he hasn't had a revelation," Mormons working against the ERA may not be campaigning as they were.[13]

On the one hand, the fact that Sonia was a woman made her particularly challenging because she pointed out, both directly and by sheer contrast, the maleness of the priesthood. She believed that the church's anti-ERA policy had been created by men with no input from women. She told listeners that "no women hold serious decision-making positions. All the managerial positions are held by men, and we don't really have any say about the policies that affect us." [14] As she articulated in particularly damaging terms before her excommunication, Sonia believed that her critiques frightened and angered the men of the church; her "unforgivable" offense was that "I'm an uppity woman, I'm politically powerful and against them."[15] She challenged the authority of male church leaders to speak about issues relating to women simply because the leaders were men. On the other hand, for many Mormons, Sonia lacked authority to question the church's position because she did not hold the priesthood simply because she was a woman. For Sonia, the fact that she was a woman was precisely what gave her the authority to speak about the ERA because the ERA was about women— their civil, constitutional, and human rights and exactly what threatened church priesthood authorities so deeply.

Although Sonia denied that she challenged church doctrine, her critiques did raise thorny theological issues about revelation and the nature of prophetic and priesthood authority. She told one audience, "I don't know if [continuing revelation has] ever been defined."[16] This ambiguity made it difficult to discern which of the prophet's words and ideas regarding the ERA were his own opinion, which were church policy, which were divinely inspired, and which were formal revelations. Sonia also found that members' faith in a policy lacking official revelatory status was "kind of a new phenomenon in the church. . . . We're believing now in revelation by implication."[17] Here, Sonia publicly questioned not only prophetic authority but also the merit of members' belief in it.

Sonia wanted the onus to be placed on individuals to get spiritual confirmation of their own beliefs, independent of the prophet's stance, like she did. "That just simply has to be what we do. We have to check out everything, we have to have the manifestation of spirit that the things we're told to do are right. . . . We can't grow simply by obedience."[18] Although Sonia sometimes invited her listeners to seek spiritual guidance about the ERA independent of the prophet's, she nonetheless maintained that she never tried to convert other LDS women to her position, only to expose the church's role in members' activism. "I never tried to get anybody to follow me, to get anyone to believe the way I believed."[19] She maintained that she stayed out of the religious territory that rightly belonged to church leaders. For many LDS observers, however, not only was Sonia challenging priesthood authority; she was trying to usurp it. She decided for herself that the church's position was wrong and did not keep this position to herself. She publicly challenged the authority of the prophet and encouraged others to do the same.

The issues around the revelatory status of the church's anti-ERA position were especially enflamed because the church had recently encountered opposition from within and without regarding a long-standing policy excluding Black men from its male-only priesthood. For most of its history, the LDS church barred Black men from holding the priesthood. The 1978 revelation withdrawing the priesthood ban came after a few decades of opposition to this exclusion from within and from outside of the church.[20] The members of the First Presidency reported that they had "pleaded long and earnestly in behalf of these, our faithful brethren, spending many hours in the Upper Room of the [Salt Lake City] Temple supplicating the Lord for divine guidance" on these issues.[21] In June 1978, Kimball received that guidance in the form of a revelation reversing the policy and welcoming "all of our brethren who are worthy" to priesthood service. This change was publicly presented as a revelation and its authority was clear. Not so for the church's anti-ERA stance.

The church struggled to respond to Sonia's very public challenges; church representatives only succeeded in muddying the nature of the church's position rather than clarifying it. They declined to declare the position against the ERA a revelation but characterized the church's position as divinely inspired—leaving unclear any distinction between those terms. While they declared externally that supporting the ERA was not grounds for church discipline, internally they challenged the faithfulness of pro-ERA Mormons. On a Utah television news special that aired before Sonia's excommunication, Relief Society president Barbara Smith said, for example, that the anti-ERA position leaders reached "after their prayerful and careful consideration should be the accepted standard of the church." When pressed, Smith uncomfortably refused to use the term "revelation" but firmly stated that directives to oppose the ERA had come as directives over the signature of the First Presidency. She clarified, "It isn't personal opinion when it comes that way, it's the word of the Lord." When asked if the church's position could be wrong, she responded self-assuredly, "No."[22] In a press conference immediately following Sonia's excommunication, Don LeFevre, head of public relations for the church, further muddied the waters as well when he said that members would not face church discipline for supporting the ERA but also that he could not "conceive of a faithful member not viewing the concern of the president of church as being inspired" in his opposition to the ERA.[23] Richard Lindsay, executive secretary of the SAC (the branch

of central church leadership Sonia accused of directing anti-ERA activism),
told a reporter that distinctions between policy and revealed doctrine were
"arbitrary" and that "to the normal member of our church ... any statement
that the First Presidency of the church feels sufficiently strongly about to
issue four policy statements, we would certainly consider that as inspired,
if not a revelation." He claimed that most church members accepted the
position "as a pronouncement which comes under [the] revelation of our
Heavenly Father."[24] Beverly Campbell, the most visible church representative
after Sonia's excommunication, told Associated Press reporter and believing
Mormon David Briscoe, "A lot of people say, well it's not a revelation. But
what is revelation? I believe they are inspired in the concern about this."[25]
So the church's position remained "the will of the Lord" and "the accepted
standard of the church," "inspired," and a pronouncement "under [the] revelation of Heavenly Father" but not a revelation.

In part in relation to this unclarity, Sonia declared that the women's issue
provoked by the ERA "will be the greatest crisis the church has ever faced"
in an appearance on a Utah television station just before her excommunication. She said, "If it's not dealt with soon, and creatively, and honestly, I
think that it's going to make that Black issue look like a tea party."[26] She was
quite distressed that it appeared that church leaders had pled for and had
received revelation on behalf of Black men but did not seem to be doing
either—pleading for or receiving revelation—on behalf of women. This led
Sonia to conclude that Black men mattered to church leaders more than
women simply "because they were men," indicating the secondary status
of women in the church—women did not matter enough for the prophet
to either seek or receive a revelation about their rights.[27]

More problematically, Sonia believed that much of the church community, women activists especially, *behaved* as though the church's position
was a revelation and their spiritual worthiness depended on following the
prophet. Evidence suggests Sonia had good reasons for this conviction. In
an address intended for all the women of the church, the Women's Fireside at the church's October 1978 Semiannual General Conference, the
same month the First Presidency released its call to activism against the
ERA, newly appointed Young Women president Elaine Q. Cannon advised
LDS women that "personal opinions may vary. Eternal principles never
do. When the prophet speaks, sisters, the debate is over."[28] This speech was
reprinted for all church members in the November 1978 *Ensign*.

At the VACC organizing meeting that same month, Campbell (not yet a church representative) framed opposing the ERA not in terms of the amendment's political failings but in terms of belief in Kimball's prophetic authority. Her logic was that although no one *demanded* that LDS women take an anti-ERA position, following the prophet meant that LDS women simply *would* take an anti-ERA stand. Less than a year later, Kimball's first counselor, N. Eldon Tanner, endorsed Cannon's statement in the August 1979 *Ensign*. Tanner promised "those who heed [the] council" of the prophet "blessings which will not be enjoyed by those who fail to accept his message" and warned of "spiritual death" to those who "fail to heed the warning voice of the prophets."[29] Historian D. Michael Quinn claims that even though the ERA was never mentioned in either Cannon's speech or Tanner's article, it was the implied backdrop and context for both.[30]

The axioms "When the prophet speaks, the debate is over" or "When the prophet speaks, the thinking has been done" rapidly became catch phrases in the debate over the question of revelation. Anti-ERA LDS women sometimes used the phrase internally as the main reason for their opposition to the ERA while publicly also defending their independence and agency. Additionally, the last section of the March 1980 Gray Book, titled "The Latter-day Saint Perspective," was a two-page appeal for church members to follow the prophet's council and clarified the meaning of the legal arguments that preceded it. It quoted several previous church leaders, from the prophet Joseph Smith to the apostle Paul to Wilford Woodruff, fourth president of the church, to George Q. Cannon, Woodruff's first counselor. These quotations enjoined readers to follow their prophet, instructed them that he would never lead them astray, and warned them against the "spiritual loss" that accompanied disobedience. As LDS scholar Martha Sonntag Bradley said, "The implication was that one could disagree, but that disagreement demonstrated a serious flaw in one's spiritual health."[31] While church leaders clarified that one *could* support the ERA and retain church membership, they also made it quite clear that believing members *would* follow the prophet instead. Anything else put in doubt one's faith in prophetic authority and, by extension, the church itself. O. Kendall White observed in a 1984 article that by the end of 1978, Mormons had little doubt of the "religious significance of their anti-ERA campaign."[32] Scholar Neil J. Young points out as well that for many LDS women, opposing the ERA was a kind of litmus test that "allowed [Mormons] to demonstrate to each other their right standing with the church through their obedience to its directives, both religious and political, and to signal to themselves and to others their 'exalted' destiny in the afterlife."[33] For women like these, coming to their own conclusions about the ERA and obeying the prophet's directive seemed to be the same thing. For them, lines between religious and political rationales were thin, if they existed at all. Whereas Sonia saw the women being manipulated by the men, the women saw themselves as following their own conscience. To them, following the prophet did not impede their political freedom—they *chose* to follow the prophet.

Sonia, on the other hand, told listeners at the American Psychological Association conference shortly before her excommunication that "in the Church there is little dialog or real education. Indoctrination is the prime method of instruction because obedience is the contemporary Church's prime message."[34] For her, thinking for oneself and opposing the ERA simply because the prophet told them to were diametrically opposed, mutually exclusive imperatives. She said, "If you believe that the leader of church is prophet . . . and he says do thus and such in politics, . . . you have to decide, am I going to go with my natural political feelings . . . or am I going to say, well, I'd rather be a good member of the church and give that up. If you give that up, you've lost some political freedom."[35] Referencing Cannon's statement and Tanner's reinforcement, she clarified, "There's a contradiction there about saying 'Well, we make up our own minds but when leaders speak debate is over. I mean, you've got to have it one way or the other."[36] For her, Cannon's widely repeated statement "doesn't leave you a lot of freedom to choose not to" oppose the ERA.[37] At least one talk show host called Sonia's bluff on this point, claiming that surely many LDS women decide for themselves whether to follow the church's position. Sonia replied, "Some of them do. I think that a great many of them however, the ones I've talked to . . . they say, 'What do you mean? You think I'm acting like a sheep, I didn't make up my own mind? . . . I prayed and I was inspired to know that the prophet's view is true.' And I say, 'Well, that's what you're supposed to do, and what would you do if the prophet changed his mind tomorrow?' 'I'd follow the prophet!' Almost without exception."[38] If church leaders clarified that the church's position was policy, not revelation, "many people who are now very active . . . working against equal rights in all this country, would . . . feel as if they didn't have to" oppose the ERA.[39]

Church member after church member seemed to publicly confirm Sonia's conviction that women's deeply felt views were rooted more in faith in prophetic authority than in an informed understanding of the issues.[40] On one radio show, an LDS woman called in to say she resented Sonia's assumption that Mormon women did not think for themselves and quickly followed up by asking Sonia if she truly believed in the church. Sonia responded, "ERA really isn't the basic issue with you, I think. If you and I were to talk for a while, we would get down right where you did, and that is to the prophet. Do we follow the prophet on everything or don't we?" A few calls later, another LDS woman stated, "Either this man is a prophet of the Lord or he isn't, it's just as simple as that." "No, it isn't," Sonia replied. The caller continued to talk over Sonia, referencing the doctrine of continuing revelation: "If you accept the premise that this man is a living prophet of the Lord, do you not think he receives revelation every day? . . . This is the very foundation of the church."[41] For this woman, the church's anti-ERA policy counted as a revelation, whatever its official status.

After her excommunication, Sonia clarified her stance that the church's position was policy, not revelation: "Since I've been excommunicated, the PR department in the church keeps saying to all the reporters who call them, it's alright for people to support the ERA. . . . That means, of course, that it was just a policy, it's proved that it was not a revelation. We [Mormons] can't tell members to go against a revelation from God."[42] For Sonia, this confirmed the conclusion she had made from the beginning: that the ERA was a political question, not a religious one—leaving her free to oppose and expose the church's anti-ERA activities while remaining a member in good standing.

The Unholy Alliance of Religion and Politics

Increasingly after Sonia's excommunication, church representatives made the revelatory status of the church's position on the ERA an individual decision, though one with spiritual consequences, not an institutional one. When Associated Press reporter David Briscoe asked Beverly Campbell in January 1980 where the church's position left a believer like him who supported the ERA, Campbell did not answer, instead reversing the question to ask Briscoe what he thought. Shortly after, Don LeFevre, also present at the interview and sometimes helping or correcting Campbell, jumped in to echo remarks he had made at the press conference following Sonia's excommunication. He told Briscoe, "I think that's up to the individual. Where are you coming from? Are you a believing faithful member of the church who looks upon President Kimball as an inspired prophet? I look at President Kimball and say, well, he must have made this a matter of prayerful consideration for a long time, he and his associates. I can't believe that concern is not inspired."[43] Here, as in the press conference, LeFevre tacitly implied that although one's position on the ERA was a matter of individual conscience, a believing member whose conscience led them to support the ERA lacked faith in the prophet's inspired position.

Thus, one of Sonia's central critiques spoke to an exercise of religion *as* politics that confused the two arenas in ways Sonia found unethical, if not unholy. For her, in taking a position on the ERA, widely believed to be at least divinely inspired, church leaders transformed a political issue into a religious one, and their patriarchal religious authority into political power—power they exercised over their members and, if successful, the entire nation. In her December 1979 *Washington Post* article published just a few weeks after her excommunication, Sonia wrote that the church's "decisive crossing over into anti-ERA politics has eroded in most members' minds the crucial distinction between church and state that our Constitution guarantees."[44] They thus exercised political dominion over LDS women that they had no right to exercise as religious leaders. That is, they demanded that LDS women substitute religious faith in the men of the church for their own political convictions about the ERA.

Sonia found this unholy alliance of religion and politics "a dangerous position" because "there's hardly an issue that comes before voters and before legislatures which isn't in some way a moral issue." She wondered "if we will feel the same pressures to conform about all subsequent moral issues as we are about the Equal Rights Amendment."[45] Sonia believed that if the church succeeded at their political machinations, it would have tremendous power over the political opinions of its members and unprecedented power over the political direction of the nation as a whole. In this case, the bulk of church members enlisted to fight against the ERA were women, already made "bootlickers and toadies" to the men, and the object of church politics was the ERA, doubling the gendered implications of male priesthood authority—LDS men were mobilizing LDS women against their own interests. For Sonia, the outgrowth of the church's involvement in the

ERA was its exercise of political control over its women under the guise of religion.

The church's involvement in LDS women's anti-ERA activism exposed the church's incomplete transition to a more limited vision of religion as a private matter separate from politics and subordinate to the state. More than any other issue in the twentieth century, the ERA made especially visible that the church continued to mix religion with politics, the spiritual with the temporal in ways Sonia found distressing enough to publicly criticize. Initially, the church declared that the ERA was "a moral, rather than a political issue," though one that would have to be "worked out in the political arena." It later conceded that the ERA had "both political and moral aspects" but emphasized its moral implications in materials printed for an LDS readership.[46] In this sense, church leaders acknowledged a difference between moral and political issues, between the authority they claimed as religious leaders and the authority they claimed not to exercise as political leaders. As I outlined in chapter 2, over time, church rhetoric shifted to include matters most people would likely consider more political than moral or religious.

Several days after Sonia's excommunication, the church appointed Beverly Campbell, cochair of the VACC, as an official church spokesperson on the ERA, a mantle she reluctantly accepted.[47] After the first few months in her role after she had honed her skills, Campbell savvily deemphasized the church's language of morality in her public appearances. Instead, she distanced the church from LDS women's activism, claiming that "the church itself is not involved politically in opposing ratification, although it encourages members as individuals to work against it."[48] She deemphasized the church's position as a motivating factor for LDS women's activism, emphasizing instead a misguided interpretation of the legal implications of the ERA. Many of the church's claims, and so Campbell's claims, reiterated many earlier claims made by anti-ERA attorney and activist Phyllis Schlafly, LDS attorney Rex E. Lee, and Harvard legal scholar Paul A. Freund.[49] In a rather alarmist vision of what domestic relations law would look like after the ERA, a vision echoed in the Gray Book, Campbell argued that the ERA could require that women contribute 50 percent of any family income, release husbands and fathers from any financial obligation to their wives and children, desegregate all single-gender spaces and athletics, subject wives, mothers, and widows to the military draft, legalize homosexuality and abortion, and legalize sexual crimes. Even a cursory reading of the congressional debates and the court cases these conservative opponents often referenced reveals that their interpretations of legislative intent and judicial history are strikingly alarmist, deceptive, and simply inaccurate. Campbell made these arguments, nonetheless, and her strategy shifted the terms of debate from whether the church's anti-ERA position was or was not a revelation to whether the church was inappropriately involved in politics.[50]

One difficulty of the church's position became clear in January 1980, during one of Campbell's earliest appearances as church spokesperson on the ERA. In a January 17, 1980 interview with Paul Swenson of *Utah Holiday* magazine (for which Don LeFevre was also present), Campbell declared that there was an "easy dividing line between this issue and the political elements of this issue." This line, however, relied on a very narrow definition of the "political" as merely having to do with candidates for elected office. The church, she said, did not involve itself in electoral politics.[51] Campbell made this claim despite the fact that in some states, information had circulated in church lobbies about candidates' positions on the ERA, and in others, petitions indicating signatories' refusal to vote for pro-ERA candidates were posted. On the same date (recordings indicate it was immediately after) in the aforementioned interview with David Briscoe, Campbell again unintentionally exposed the slippage between morality and politics in the church's position. It was even more difficult for Campbell to respond when Briscoe asked her what morality informed the church's opposition to extending the time to pass the ERA. After some fumbling around, Campbell implied that any law could be framed as political but only some laws as moral. Frustrated, she simply stated, "You can't separate the two. Do you see?"[52]

Some observers noted the ambiguity inherent in Campbell's position as a church representative articulating the problems with the ERA in terms most people would consider political. On a January episode of *Contact* hosted by Craig Clyde, one audience member told Campbell he was "still struggling with your role in this. . . . If this is really a moral position, and the church is stating this as a moral issue, why did they send legal representative rather than ecclesiastical one to discuss this topic with us?" Campbell's response elided the point of the admittedly poorly framed question by simply replying, "I'm not an attorney, so I am not a legal representative." In a rhetorical sleight of hand, she elided the issue of religion and politics simply by changing its terms. She responded, "I have expressed to the leadership of the church that I do feel that this is a women's issue and that women should address this issue." Campbell was there representing the church not as a legal representative but because she was a woman. The relevant question, Campbell implied here and elsewhere, was not about religion and political authority but about gender and power.[53] She declared, "Women do have great role in the church. . . . In fact I don't think there's any church where women have as significant a role in the body of the church. . . . We don't have any women bishops or apostles, and again that's a doctrinal thing, and I have no problems with that, and I don't think most women do."[54] Her tacit intimation was that the women Sonia thought were being controlled by the men of the church actually had considerable power in the church, so Sonia had no right to the sorts of complaints she was making.

As historian J. Spencer Fluhman points out, some observers have noticed many contexts in which the church seems to deploy "one language for outsiders and another for those within the fold."[55] I might add that what nonmembers hear and what members hear in the very same language are often different things, frequently by design. This may have been the case when it came to the ERA. To outsiders, Campbell largely appeared to be making political claims for their own sake, though informed by moral concerns about the family. To LDS listeners, though, the moral and religious implications of Campbell's claims were likely clear by virtue of church rhetoric in meetings and publications like the Gray Book. For this reason, the church's more political reasoning looked to Sonia like it merely gave women the political language to help them do as Beers suggested at the VACC organizing meeting: to speak to senators not in the religious terms motivating their objections to the ERA but in legal language that might sway legislators' votes.[56]

In some ways, Sonia's critiques of LDS activism was informed by a secularist position advocating a strict separation of church and state. Much more frequently, though, Sonia acknowledged (even if she did not like) the church's right to campaign against the ERA. Her problem was more that the church hid its politics behind religion. She thought that while the church acted as though it maintained a distinction between religion and politics and stayed in its lane, in practice it collapsed the one into the other, taking over the whole road. Church leaders' "gravest error" was "denying that they were doing those things. I mean if they had come out and said, 'Sure, why can't we do this?' and been above board and open . . . then I don't know that there would have been anything seriously wrong with it."[57] In Sonia's view, these denials were intimately related to why the church refused to publicly declare its ERA position a revelation but seemed to expect members to treat it as such behind the scenes. She said the church "can't expect to hide behind their ecclesiastical skirt. They can't expect to go out into politics like this and then say 'Oh, we're going to affect public policy but we're going to be awful private about it. And we don't want anybody to say anything mean to us about what we're doing because we're a church.'"[58] She wanted the church to engage in politics honestly and fairly.

Sonia also believed that since the church had chosen to enter the political arena by organizing its women, she and her supporters were justified in their political responses. She maintained a strict boundary between religion and politics and so could view her criticisms of the church as criticisms of a political organization, not a religion, and of church leaders as political actors, not representatives of God. She said, "I never did deny the prophet, and I don't now. The only reason I came into conflict with church is because it didn't only have a policy against [the ERA], it is actively fighting it and organizing people against it."[59] She advocated that in response to church activism, pro-ERA activists of all faiths oppose the church on political fronts: "Just give them heck. Pressure 'em, lobby 'em, just do all kinds of things to them that you would do with anybody that opposed you. . . . See the church as political entity and be willing, now, to go forward and do something about it."[60]

In the months after her excommunication, Sonia maintained that her controversial statement that NOW members in Kalispell should tell church leaders that they were refusing to speak to missionaries because of the church's anti-ERA position was offered in this vein—it was political, not religious. She said, "I don't know how much difference this distinction makes to Mormons, but it makes a lot of difference to me."[61] She believed that because the church was a proselytizing church, "perhaps the only lever they had for deal-making . . . is the church's earnest desire to have all non-members listen to its missionary members."[62] For her, this was "simple *quid pro quo* lobbying—if you'll listen to me, I'll listen to you. I'll listen to your missionaries if you'll unhand my equal rights."[63] Church leaders, however, saw her statement as doing harm to the missionary program in religious terms, as Willis's excommunication letter suggested.

Sonia never seriously questioned the church's right to excommunicate her; she knew that churches were not states and that churches have the right to regulate the boundaries of their membership.[64] Rather, for Sonia, the most relevant question was whether her excommunication was warranted on religious or doctrinal terms. In her mind, nothing in LDS doctrine justified the church's position against the ERA, so "this is political." The ostensibly religious court was no more than a political witch hunt.[65] Sonia viewed her excommunication as one instance of the church avoiding accountability for its politics by virtue of identifying Sonia's political offenses as religious ones. She and all LDS women "shouldn't have to choose between your church and your politics."[66] Hence, not only was it nonsensical to excommunicate someone from a religion for political reasons; it was also immoral—the church was using religion to try to silence her political voice by excommunicating her. As she said in the *Washington Post* a few weeks after her excommunication, the church was "distorting evidence in order to rid itself of political opposition."[67] These "unfortunate distortions came about largely, I believe, because of Bishop Willis's insistence upon wrenching all statements and actions in question out of the political context in which they occurred, and forcing them into a religious context for which they were never intended and in which they cease entirely to reflect my opinions."[68] Sonia believed that had the church simply admitted that it had become a political organization as well as a religious institution, and had it expected to be treated as such, she would not have been excommunicated. Many observers agreed, but Campbell did not.

Campbell's public role as the church's representative on the ERA often required her to answer questions about Sonia's excommunication, so Campbell's public appearances, along with a rare press conference or remark from church authorities, are the closest we have to an official church position on many of the issues swirling around LDS anti-ERA activism and Sonia's excommunication. Campbell pointed out that Sonia's accusation that church leaders practiced a "savage misogyny" had not been in the context of the ERA. Campbell conceded that "in the speech, she talked about them as part of American society, but in the trial she was asked specifically if she was referring to them."[69] She was, though Campbell failed to point out that Sonia was including them in a larger culture of misogyny. When confronted with this point, Campbell clarified, "It doesn't matter whether you're talking about all of society or when you narrow it down to those specific people, it's just as damaging."[70]

More to the point, though, Campbell identified a different set of reasons for Sonia's excommunication, some of them beyond those in Sonia's excommunication letter (see chapter 2), that had very little to do with the ERA and much more to do with church patriarchy. Campbell zoned in on Sonia's critiques of church leaders specifically and of patriarchy more broadly, pointing to the doctrinal stakes of Sonia's critique of LDS patriarchal leadership. Sonia's error was that she "felt that she needed to develop doctrine and ideas that were contrary to these basic principles [of patriarchal church leadership]."[71] After hearing of Sonia's personal revelation that "patriarchy is a sham," Campbell declared, "If your own personal voices tell you that patriarchy is a sham, that's a doctrinal difference, that's not an ERA difference."[72] She also claimed that Sonia's APA paper represented Sonia's position that the women's movement "will be the death cry of the patriarchy" and showed that "she wants to see this whole system [the church] destroyed."[73] For her, that Sonia's critiques appeared in the context of the ERA did not matter. "If you're talking about church doctrine, and you are flaunting your disagreement with basic church doctrine, . . . that's where it's coming from regardless of the context."[74] The ERA was simply a "peg to hang these differences on."[75] For Campbell, and perhaps for church leaders responsible for her excommunication, these larger critiques of patriarchal leadership were how Sonia "excommunicated herself."[76]

Sonia wanted to have it both ways: she claimed that the church improperly mixed politics with religion but that her critiques were limited to one and not the other. It was on this knife edge that Sonia negotiated her public criticisms of the church she believed in and loved. Her conviction that her position was merely political allowed her to evade the theological implications of her critiques. In her view, she was excommunicated because she opposed church leaders' political positions repeatedly, out loud and in public, and she encouraged others to do so. However, the church also wanted to have it both ways. It maintained it was not a political organization and viewed Sonia's critiques as primarily religious, even while it engaged in politics behind the scenes. On this knife edge, as John Unger Zussman and

Shauna M. Adix observe, the decision to excommunicate Sonia "attempted to delineate a fine line between supporting the ERA in opposition to the church and opposing the church in support of the ERA."[77] The church's position required church leaders and representatives to deflect, deny, or keep secret its level of involvement in organizing LDS women against the ERA. Chapter 4 explores some of the gendered implications of the church's evasions and deceptions as Sonia saw them.

CHAPTER FOUR

"The Grossest Misuses of Women's Religious Convictions"

Gender, Honesty, and Accountability

Pervading throughout and among the issues of prophetic authority, church patriarchy, and religion and politics discussed in chapter 3 were questions Sonia raised about honesty, secrecy, and accountability under church patriarchy. Sonia used her notoriety to argue to anyone who would listen that church leaders used their religious authority not only to remake women's religious belief into political opinion but also to hide behind the women of the church, instructing them to lie about who organized them and whom they represented. Sonia accused the church of hiding behind LDS women's "civic" organizations and believed that church leaders required women's dishonesty to cover their own tracks and hide responsibility for their own politics. That is, the women of the church fronted for the men so the men could avoid accountability. Sonia found this simply "diabolical."[1] This chapter investigates these accusations with an eye to what they suggest about gender, agency, and power in the church.

The Men Organizing the Women

From the very beginning, Sonia told anyone who would listen that church leaders in Salt Lake City were running a centralized, coordinated anti-ERA campaign by secretly organizing its women into lobbying groups like the VACC that only *looked* local. In truth, she claimed, "the directions to do what is happening on the local level have come from Salt Lake City, from an office called the Special Affairs Committee, and they are like a political action committee in the church." The church was "organizing, through the headquarters of the church in Salt Lake, all down through the hierarchy of the church. . . . They really became political activists."[2] Citizens councils like the VACC, Sonia contended, were extensions of church patriarchy in all but name.

The citizens councils did seem to have close ties with the church. The VACC's co-organizer, Regional Representative Don Ladd, told Linda Sillitoe that the line between the church and the VACC was "fine."[3] Bill Evans, assistant to the SAC, also told Sillitoe that because the ERA was a moral and not a political issue, the citizens council in Missouri "and others in other states are overseen by the [Special Affairs] Committee."[4] Looking back on the ERA years, Rodney P. Foster, assistant secretary in the First Presidency's office, told historian D. Michael Quinn in 1992 that the activism of the councils was done under the authority of "what they now call Special Affairs."[5] More locally, it also seems clear that, at least in Virginia, Hinckley had, in fact, asked Regional Representative Julian Lowe to set up the VACC. Lowe's niece, Kathryn MacKay, testified at Sonia's excommunication trial that her uncle told her such.[6] Lowe himself also confirmed this in an interview with Linda Sillitoe.[7] These facts seem to demonstrate significant contributions, at the very least, of the men of the church to the women's citizens councils.

More important to Sonia was her related claim that in addition to organizing the women, the men also told the women what to think, say, and do. Sonia claims that the VACC and organizations like it elsewhere "had countless meetings before they did anything, to be told by the men what to do."[8] Sonia also claimed that during the letter-writing campaigns conducted during Relief Society and other gatherings, church leaders told the women when to write, to whom, and what to say. Although likely overstated, there seems to be at least some merit to this claim. D. Michael Quinn points out that in at least one instance, shortly after Apostle and SAC member Boyd K. Packer gave Nevada women an assignment to write their congressional representatives, legislators received four thousand such letters in one day.[9] In other instances, Relief Societies held meetings and socials at which they wrote anti-ERA letters to legislators, sometimes following a provided template. For Sonia, this sort of behavior amounted to a large-scale campaign of deception in which women represented the anti-ERA positions of the men of the church as their own.

While Sonia frequently expressed outrage at church leaders' role in directing women's activism, she found herself powerless to stop it. Early on, she discovered that although she could not get the church to admit to its role in ERA politics, she could pressure the VACC to do so. Virginia law required that any organization spending over one hundred dollars for the purpose of influencing legislators must register as a lobbying group. Shortly after the VACC was organized, it failed to do so. Sonia clarified to the secretary of the commonwealth, Frederick T. Gray, that the group had spent over two thousand dollars printing pamphlets, buttons, bumper stickers, and "concern sheets." Coalition leaders disagreed about where those funds came from and where those materials went and whether they needed to register or not. The cochair of the VACC, Jean Zundel, said that nearly three-fourths of the printed pamphlets had gone to legislators and that the organization had earlier decided that Campbell should register it, but she never did.[10] According to Sonia, the organization was investigated and registered only after a Virginia reporter for a local newspaper ran a headline, "State Official Probes Mormon Lobbying."[11]

When controversy erupted, Campbell was frequently called on to defend this failure. She said that much of the printing was donated and very little of it went to legislators, so the organization did not meet the one-hundred-dollar threshold. She also said that she had initially contacted the secretary of the commonwealth's office and asked if the VACC needed to register and was told they did not. There "was no investigation." After Sonia's accusation made headlines, church representative Beverly Campbell "did go down and meet with the secretary of the commonwealth, I said, ' . . . why don't we register because I don't want any problems.'"[12] This might have remained a local issue discussed primarily in Virginia newspapers had Sonia not continued to discuss it in several public appearances across the country to illustrate the church's duplicity.[13]

Campbell's involvement with the VACC was likely one reason she was selected to represent the church regarding the ERA and may have increased her credibility with some listeners. In response to Sonia's accusations, Campbell at times denied any relationship whatsoever between the church and the councils—they did "not fit into the general structure of the church. We use ward and stake structures as they exist, but we use those lines only because they exist."[14] For her, because organizations like the

VACC were not organizationally incorporated into the formal hierarchy of church leadership, they were distinct from the church itself. For Campbell, formal organizational structure trumped less official lines of communication and organization. Campbell also contended that the church did not control LDS women activists and so was not involved in their campaigns against the ERA; the women did it on their own.

At other times, though, Campbell admitted and defended the church's organizing role: "If [the church has] a moral position and . . . does not provide some kind of opportunities for a forum, then that would be a real concern."[15] She told Paul Swenson that the request for her to help establish the VACC came directly from Regional Representative Lowe, though she pointed out that she could have refused it.[16] More frequently, she framed the role of the church in LDS women's activism by limiting the church's involvement to the mere declaration of its position. Campbell repeatedly denied the involvement of leaders in Salt Lake City in the citizens councils, denying in particular that Hinckley was behind the organization of the VACC.[17]

Campbell's denials distinguished between the First Presidency and the Quorum of the Twelve in Salt Lake City and more local leaders, like regional representatives, stake presidents, and bishops. While Campbell consistently denied any direction coming out of Salt Lake City, she was more divided about local leaders. On the one hand, she "would love to say that it was the men who are fighting the amendment. That would be marvelous because we certainly need their help," but the women organized themselves.[18] However, in response to Sonia's claim that LDS women were merely following men's direction, Campbell said, "I think what Sonia is referring to is the fact that a regional representative [likely Lowe] said that . . . the president of our church said this is something that we would like to see done."[19] She continued to say that Lowe had asked her "if I would like to take the lead. I indeed said yes. I think that's . . . a very proper kind of thing for a regional representative to do."[20] She also acknowledged that the VACC kept Lowe apprised of their activities, but "we do not look for direct counsel and advice in execution of the council."[21] However, she continued that "the nature of the things we do . . . would certainly not be contrary to having a priesthood advisor. . . . I think that's a concept, you know, if you're a member of the church, you feel very comfortable with." So while Campbell denied any role for priesthood leaders in the VACC, she was quite comfortable with the general concept of priesthood leadership of women's political activism. She believed that if coalition members were also church members, they would want to be sure of the church's position so they would not "be out of line." Campbell contended that if a citizens council had "LDS" in its name, as the VACC did, it must at the very least accurately represent the church's position.[22]

Campbell also admitted a more limited role for local priesthood leaders in some states. For example, the day after Sonia's appearance on a Saint Louis radio program, Campbell told the same show's listeners that in Missouri, "men have not been a party to the planning of the [Missouri Citizens] council."[23] Within days, though, she told another reporter that she was "not absolutely certain as to how it's done in Missouri or how it's organized. I think that indeed if it is organized with a priesthood advisor then that's very appropriate."[24] Campbell conceded that the Missouri Citizens Council received more priesthood direction than the VACC but noted that council leaders in Missouri asked for it.[25]

Nonetheless, the church's role in LDS women's activism felt dishonest to Sonia. It concerned her deeply that the church maintained a false image as a religious organization while hiding the responsibility for its politics behind the veneer of women's citizens councils. Through the councils, Sonia stated, the church's highly organized and hierarchical priesthood structure allowed Mormons, who were "a tiny, non-representative, highly organized and highly motivated minority, directed by religious leaders in Utah and for the most part not by their own independent, informed convictions, [to] privately [affect] public policy out of all proportion to their numbers."[26] This "exaggerates, *wildly*, the size of the anti-ERA opinion."[27] By misleading congressional representatives about their motivations at the behest of church leaders, LDS women could convince legislators that they acted from their own conviction and represented a majority of similarly minded citizens. In Sonia's view, neither was true. For her, this deception put the church itself in moral peril: "We [MERA] consider it not only morally reprehensible, but politically unfair for ERA proponents to have to fight an invisible enemy," one hiding behind the women's citizens councils.[28] The church, she argued, was analogous to termites, invisibly but ubiquitously eating away at the foundation of women's rights.[29]

The question of the church's role in local political activism took particular shape among Mormons around a controversy over whether church activists (and Campbell herself as chair of the VACC) were "called" to or "set apart" for their activist roles, an issue that received quite a bit of attention in the local press in Utah, among members who understood its significance. Initially, Sonia accused the church of issuing formal priesthood "callings" to Beverly Campbell and perhaps other women activists in Virginia and elsewhere to campaign against the ERA. In the LDS church, a "calling" is a church leadership position and a religious obligation bestowed by male priesthood leaders. Sonia clarified that this "means that hands were laid on [Campbell's] head, [she was] called by the men . . . as a priesthood duty to do this," adding fuel to the accusation that men organized the women of the VACC, who then functioned as representatives of the church disguised as private citizens.[30] Whether LDS activists were "called" to their positions mattered because it spoke to Sonia's claims about the church's role in directing the activism of its members. If women were "called" to their position, this would have indicated some level of priesthood involvement in and authority over women's activism.

The women in the VACC organizing committee who asked for callings knew the value of callings and sought such endorsement in the VACC organizing meeting. During the meeting, Campbell had told the women in attendance, "You have got to take this seriously as a calling."[31] Campbell continued to say that a major rally would occur on November 19 (presumably the one at the state legislature in Richmond) and that "we were called on Sunday to do this job," presumably by the October 12, 1978 letter from the First Presidency inviting members to activism. In response, one attendee asked if the women activists would be formally called and set apart. A discussion ensued in which many women expressed a desire for a calling to "know for a surety" that their activism was church sanctioned."[32] Campbell told attendees, "Without being set apart, I will do what is appropriate to do because the prophet has asked me to do it. I don't need any of the rest of that and I don't think any of the rest of us here do either."[33] For Campbell and likely for many attendees, whether the calling was a formal one mattered little. However, Campbell told Paul Swenson that in Virginia, the decision not to make any anti-ERA roles formal callings was made early because "it's a citizens council."[34] Campbell conceded that she had asked for and received a priesthood blessing, a ritual intended to provide spiritual guidance to its recipient but with no structural relationship to callings in the institutional church.[35] Regardless, the minutes of the VACC organizing meeting indicate that Campbell and Lowe both used the language of "callings" liberally, claiming that whether they had received a formal calling or not, the women should *act* as if they had one.

When Utah reporter Linda Sillitoe investigated church anti-ERA activism, though, she found a different picture in Missouri that Sonia undoubtedly knew. Sillitoe's findings gave some legitimacy to Sonia's claims that activists were "called" by the church when she reported that members of the Missouri Citizens Council "were given 'priesthood callings' to work as 'private citizens'" against the ERA.[36] In the wake of controversy, church leaders ceased formally calling women to ERA activism nationwide, and the issue simply fizzled out.[37] What was at stake in this controversy was that if women were either officially or informally called to their anti-ERA activism, then church leaders, formally or informally, played at least some role in directing women's activism. In this sense, Sonia pointed out, although anti-ERA organizations were not structurally incorporated into the institutional church, LDS women and priesthood leaders alike *acted* as though they were.

While the controversy over callings faded away, public discussion of whether the church was organizing against the ERA did not, and Campbell frequently had to account for it. She frequently told listeners that LDS women activists responded to the First Presidency's call to activism not as church representatives but as private citizens. According to her logic, when Lowe and Ladd invited and worked with Campbell to organize the VACC (most likely at Hinckley's request), they were acting as private citizens. When young men in the church distributed anti-ERA materials as part of a church-organized service project, when bishops asked church members to donate funds during or outside of church meetings and buildings, when believers posted and signed anti-ERA petitions in church lobbies, when members used existing organizational church leadership structures to plan and conduct political activities, or when local church leaders or members organized, raised money for, and/or privately paid for buses to take Relief Society women to the state legislature to lobby, they all acted as private citizens. This distinction between church representative and private citizens allowed church representatives to claim that the church was not at all behind women's activism; members' political actions were distinct from their religious convictions. This logic enabled church members to campaign politically on religious grounds and enabled church leaders to appear above the fray of politics. For Sonia, though, "when Mormons try to tell you that they are just acting as concerned citizens, and they're not organized for the church, that is not true. . . . The very structure of the church is being used against the equal rights amendment."[38]

The dispute over in which capacity Mormon church leaders and members acted, as church representatives or as private citizens, was particularly evident in two controversies over how LDS activism was funded: the "washing" of funds to support LDS women's anti-ERA organizations and the raising of money in the spring of 1980 in California for state senate campaigns in Florida. Each made headlines, the first locally and the second nationally. Sonia pointed to these two related controversies frequently, finding them underhanded enough to merit significant concern and mentioned them frequently to the press and to her listeners.

Before her excommunication, Sonia told her listeners that in several states, local bishops asked members for donations which went to innocuously named organizations like Families Are Concerned Today (FACT) in Virginia, Citizens for Family Life in Iowa and Illinois, Save Our Families Today in Tennessee, Quest for Quality Government in Nevada, Friends of the Family in North Carolina, A Better Way in Georgia, and others.[39] Sonia called FACT "a money washing kind of thing, so that it wouldn't look as if the church were [sic] really spending church moneys. And in fact it wasn't . . . as far as we know."[40] Linda Sillitoe pointed out that although VACC officers called FACT "an organization that raises funds," Sillitoe could find no fundraising events or membership lists for it. "It was, all told, a bank account" that "serve[d] no obvious purpose except to disguise the structure of revenue."[41] As Sonia saw it, these funds were solicited by church leaders and accepted in church houses, and donations were likely made out of religious rather than political sentiments. She was clear that local priesthood leaders raised funds for anti-ERA activity at the direction of central church leaders in Salt Lake City. Sonia also knew that most members understood that the church wanted financial support for its anti-ERA campaigns, whatever the logistical means by which donations were requested and made. For these reasons, she claimed that the church raised thousands of dollars through these accounts while claiming it was not raising money at all.

Campbell agreed with Sonia that "categorically, in all matters of which I have knowledge, which is probably as much as anyone, never has one dime of church money been used."[42] However, she more carefully phrased her denials that local bishops had asked members for donations. In one of Campbell's first public appearances as official church spokesperson, when asked if the church directed its members to contribute funds for anti-ERA activism, she responded, "Not that I'm aware of."[43] In another interview, she stumbled to say she was certain that bishops who asked church members to donate did so "as individual citizens."[44] She said, "I'm sure that they were asked as individuals because either they were knowledgeable of people or— . . . I mean, you know, we all have a position in the church . . . and if you look for somebody who has no position in the church to do a job, you're going to be hard pressed to find somebody to do the job."[45] Campbell thus maintained that the councils were funded by church members who donated as private citizens at the request of church leaders also acting as private citizens.

A related controversy erupted in the spring of 1980, when money California church members raised was sent to Florida to support the campaigns of four anti-ERA candidates for the Florida state legislature. This seeming misappropriation of funds, more than the first controversy, indicated that Sonia's larger concerns about church fundraising may have had some merit. The *Miami Herald* reported on its front page that in California, bishops and other local authorities raised up to sixty thousand dollars, thirteen thousand of it in two days. They divided Northern California along church boundaries to determine which congregations' funds would support which of four anti-ERA Florida candidates.[46] The money also financed a Florida advertising blitz and paid to print and distribute 425,000 anti-ERA leaflets there.[47]

When this story broke, Jerry Cahill of the church public relations office acknowledged that "a call for Florida campaign contributions was received by church authorities in Salt Lake City, who then requested that funds be raised by church authorities in Northern California."[48] He also admitted to a *Miami Herald* reporter that "things undoubtedly were done on review that shouldn't have been done."[49] According to the *Sacramento Bee*, however, local California church officials denied that church leaders in Salt Lake City had requested the money and donating members refuted any suggestion that their contributions were made "through church auspices."[50] In their minds, private individuals who happened to be bishops and stake presidents, at the request of other private individuals who happened to be high-ranking church leaders, asked for donations from still other private citizens who happened to be church members to fund legislative campaigns in another state. According to the *Miami Herald*, "critics question whether members can make [a] distinction" between private individuals and the church positions they held. One church member told the paper, "There is no such thing as a person in authority in our church working as an individual. People don't differentiate between a person's position as an individual and that person's position as their leader, an inspired teacher of God."[51] Even though Cahill had admitted and apologized for flawed financial practices in this instance, this more local stance seemed to confirm Sonia's claims that priesthood leaders were raising money for the ERA while avoiding accountability by declaring they were merely private citizens. It seems that even while they denied it, church members understood their donations to be religious ones.

The Women Fronting for the Men

As troubling as the men organizing the women was for Sonia, she was perhaps more vexed by her sense that the men of the church asked women to lie about both who organized them and whom they represented. As I mentioned in chapter 2, at the VACC organizing meeting, Regional Representative Julian Lowe said, "We have found that it is not so good for the men to be so vociferous. It works against the *cause*. . . . If the brethren are out beating the bushes it looks like, in the eyes of some, that we are trying to keep the women subservient and it is far from that. This is the exact opposite of what we are trying to do, but it is always interpreted that way."[52] Sonia frequently misquoted Lowe's comment at the VACC meeting as saying, "'Don't tell anyone the men have organized you.' He said, 'It doesn't look good when the men are out there beating the bushes on women's issues. . . . People won't understand!'" She often assured her audiences she was "giving you the exact quote off the tape," though she clearly was not.[53] She nonetheless claimed that what Lowe's statement "means is everyone will understand exactly that this is men again using women as tools of their own oppression."[54] For Sonia, Lowe's statement amounted to an unintentional confession that despite what Campbell or any other woman said, the men of the church had organized the women to do their anti-ERA bidding. Sonia "was shocked that [the men] were telling those women to misrepresent themselves! To pretend that they had organized themselves!"[55]

Sonia said that in other instances, the women "were told that when they got down to Richmond [to lobby], if anyone asked them, 'What organization do you represent?' they were to say, they didn't represent any organization, they were just private, concerned citizens."[56] In Sonia's mind, this was a lie. She thought that LDS women lobbyists were more church representatives than private citizens because they had been told what to believe, what to say, and even how to represent themselves by the men of the church. For her, "'I am fighting the ERA because the prophet has told me to' is different from 'I have studied and come to my own personal conclusions about it and here I am wanting to oppose it.'"[57] Sonia believed that because the former statement would betray that women activists indeed spoke for the prophet and not for themselves, church leaders instructed them to say the latter instead. The result of this kind of instruction, Sonia said, was that "when they go and lobby, they say, 'I'm just a little housewife. I was standing by my sink one day and thought I'm going to go down to that legislature'" to lobby against the ERA, even though they had been sent by the men of the church.[58] LDS women were arriving by the hundreds at several state legislatures, often on buses they boarded in local church parking lots, to lobby against the ERA. Sonia believed that these women had been directed by the men to deceive legislators that they lobbied, saying they were private citizens rather than representatives of the church. For Sonia, these requests that women lie about who organized them demonstrated the moral turpitude of the church's clandestine anti-ERA activism. "Requiring members to be less than honest, for whatever purpose, must eventually be lethal to a religious body."[59] Sonia knew the women were less than honest about who they represented because, as she stated in one of her most oft-repeated sentences, "if the prophet changed his mind tomorrow, . . . those people with those badges, most of them, would no longer be in your hall lobbying."[60] For her, the women clearly represented the church's views, acting on its behalf, not their own.

The minutes of the VACC organizing meeting attribute the offending request that women lie about their motivations to Robert Beers, who advocated against asking legislators to oppose the ERA because Kimball did, but rather to "talk his [congressional representatives'] language, not yours."[61] In one public appearance, though, Campbell claimed she had said it herself. She told one interviewer, "A legislator is not interested in your religious point of view." Her logic was that although religious conviction might motivate LDS women's activism, legislators were not interested in religious motivations, only political reasons. She buttressed this claim with a moral claim of her own, that the sort of religious disclosure Sonia seemed to demand smacked of religious persecution. She said, "I think we're long since passed the time of wearing a star of David."[62] Campbell's troubling invocation of the Holocaust aside, her point was that the religion of any activist was irrelevant to their political message. For her, there was nothing at all problematic about mobilizing political rhetoric to express a religious conviction.

To Sonia, this was all smoke and mirrors meant to protect the men of the church. Most troubling was that it occurred at the expense of women. That is, church leaders across the priesthood hierarchy avoided account-ability for the church's politics by hiding behind women's skirts. In her private meeting with Hinckley and Maxwell of the SAC, Sonia asked the men "why they weren't taking responsibility for the organizations that they were helping to start in all these states and for which they were responsible, why they were allowing the women to front for them and cover for them." Maxwell accused Sonia of "driving us apart" with "very emotionally laden terms" like "front and cover." Sonia responded, "That's how I see what you are doing, is that you are making the women take the responsibility, making them cover for you."[63] From her perspective, the men of the church invited women's dishonest and unethical behaviors to avoid their own political accountability.

Sonia's problem of women "fronting" for men began with the organiza-tion of the citizens councils but surfaced most powerfully and publicly in the wake of Sonia's appearance on *Donahue* in December 1979 (which aired in most places in January or early February 1980). While filming the episode, the host, Phil Donahue, wrongly claimed that the church refused to send a representative to appear alongside Sonia, and much public con-troversy ensued. The details surrounding this series of events are contested; each of the four people involved—Sonia, general Relief Society president Barbara Smith, Beverly Campbell, and *Donahue* producer Darlene Hayes—report slightly different accounts. The most accurate narrative I can con-struct from these is that Sonia was set to appear on *Donahue* alongside a representative of the church on Wednesday, December 12, just days after her excommunication. The Friday before, Hayes had invited Smith to appear with Sonia, but one day before filming, Smith declined to appear. Smith later explained that "Johnson was already, although inaccurately, considered a martyr for women's rights and that if we appeared together on his program, what I had to say would not get proper attention." Sonia reported, however, that Hayes told her that the men in Salt Lake City would not allow Smith to appear, a claim Sonia repeated frequently. Smith suggested to Heber G. Wolsey of the Office of Public Relations of the church that he ask Campbell to appear in Smith's stead. He did and Campbell agreed.[64]

When Hayes told Sonia that the church had selected Campbell instead of a church authority of any sort to appear with her, Sonia "felt really not right about that, not right about Beverly Campbell, and I couldn't figure out exactly why." Talking out her discomfort with her friend Arlene Wood, Sonia came to three conclusions. First, Sonia thought that the church was "telling everyone that this was a local affair. . . . If they had me [on] with Beverly Campbell, it would look like it was just a fight between Virginians out there who had different opinions," minimizing the scope of the church's campaigns.[65] Sonia was unwilling to play into this tactic. Second, Sonia refused to allow the men of the church to make ERA politics look like women "just having a cat fight again" instead of a campaign the men called for and directed. She declared, "Men always like to see women fighting because it trivializes things."[66] Third, Sonia reasoned that the church sending someone in a policy- or decision-making capacity would have acknowledged the church's involvement in LDS women's anti-ERA activism. She said, "If they had me on with [Relief Society president] Barbara Smith, it would look like somehow the whole church was involved."[67] For these reasons, Sonia refused to appear with Campbell because she had no official or decision-making role in the church; she "was just a woman from Virginia, like me."[68] Sonia offered to let Campbell go on the show alone, but *Donahue* representatives told Sonia they wanted her. She realized then that "I was the one in power, the TV people wanted *me*. . . . The church was not in control, I was in control. . . . And so I decided, since I had control, I would have a man or no one."[69] Sonia appeared on the hour-long program alone.

During filming, Phil Donahue erroneously claimed that the church had refused to offer a representative for the conversation when, in fact, they had offered Campbell. Whether Campbell was appointed an official church spokesperson just before or just after the show is contested, though she may have been groomed by church leaders for the role.[70] Sonia appeared alone on the one-hour *Donahue* program. Because of the broadcast, though, Campbell became the first woman ever to serve the church in a specifically public relations role. Campbell continued to represent the church's position on the ERA to the public and respond to questions about Sonia's excommunication for the next few years.

For Sonia, this incident inaugurated a controversial personal policy she discussed often: she would welcome any opportunity to "debate any Mormon male who has any policy-making powers. Any of them! Or all of them at once."[71] But she would not debate Mormon women. As she told one Utah reporter, "It seems to me only reasonable that if you're going to debate somebody, debate somebody who had a hand in the decision and could change it if necessary."[72] When almost every interviewer after *Donahue* aired asked Sonia about her refusal to publicly appear with or debate LDS women, she explained, "I will only consent to speak with one of the men who are making the anti-ERA policies and who are organizing against the Equal Rights Amendment because it's the men who are making the decisions and the men who are fighting the amendment."[73] She was "not going to fight women, women are my sisters," a personal principle that remained with her throughout her life.[74]

Within days of Sonia's *Donahue* broadcast, Campbell appeared on television and radio talk shows in several locations airing the church's grievance about Donahue's misinformation. The most thorough of these interviews aired in Utah. Roy Gibson of KTVX and Patrick Greenlaw of KUTV, both well-known figures in Utah local news, interviewed Campbell separately on local Utah television.[75] In these interviews, Campbell publicly requested that *Donahue* representatives provide equal time for the church to discuss its position. A few weeks later, Campbell and Smith appeared together on their own full-hour *Donahue* episode. During this appearance, Smith seemed to confirm Sonia's fears that church representatives would treat women's anti-ERA activism as though it was locally organized. When asked why she had initially refused to appear with Sonia, Smith told Donahue, "I really did think very carefully and decided, well let's have someone there who can answer the questions, let's say what happened in Virginia. It's a local issue. It was not something that happened from church headquarters."[76]

Beyond *Donahue*, though, Sonia believed that Campbell's public relations campaign on behalf of the church was merely a single instance of the men of the church requiring the women of the church to articulate, promote, and defend anti-ERA policies they had no role in making and then lie about it. Sonia told Paul Swenson, "The men in the church who have been directing the anti-ERA political activity in several states can stand back and not be accountable by letting Beverly Campbell do it for them."[77] Sonia felt it only fair that the men directing LDS women's activism in Virginia and elsewhere should have to own their behavior, not hide behind Campbell's and other women's skirts. Campbell either misunderstood or misconstrued Sonia's concerns about debating Campbell or any other LDS women. She distorted Sonia's position by simplifying it, saying merely that Sonia would not appear publicly with LDS women because "her enemies are the men."[78] Campbell's evaluation of Sonia's policy not to debate Mormon women resorted a simple question of blame in place of the more complex appraisal of responsibility and deception Sonia articulated.

Many people noticed the irony of Sonia's position, at once wanting to empower LDS women and refusing to debate with them. One caller to a radio show (a man, by the sound of it) found her refusal to debate women representatives of the church "hypocritical." Sonia replied, "In this case, it [gender] isn't relevant because the people that are making the policies *just happen* to be men. If they just happened to be women, then I'd speak to them."[79] For Sonia, appearing with or debating Campbell, or any LDS woman, would do the opposite of empowering women; it would require the women to front for the men and to disguise the men's positions as their own. One interviewer noted that surely some LDS women were making independent choices to oppose the ERA and asked if, in that case, there was "anyone worthy to debate." Sonia responded that of course some LDS women were thinking for themselves, but "I thought we were talking about the ones that I would argue with," no doubt a coded dig at Campbell and Smith.[80] For Sonia, church leaders had made Campbell, sometimes Smith, and nearly all anti-ERA activists take the heat for the men's anti-ERA position, and Sonia was having none of it.

Sonia felt a kinship with the LDS women who she thought had been asked to campaign against their own interests and lie about it because "I was one of them."[81] For Sonia, "when a church begins to exploit the testimonies of members for its political purposes, that organization, if it's a religion, is in serious, serious moral trouble."[82] In her view, this was "the grossest misuses of women's religious convictions that I have ever heard of. . . . It is really diabolical . . . that women's deep religious emotions are being used against them."[83] It was "spiritual blackmail."[84] Church leaders' "telephones and their mailboxes ought to be flooded with outrage at what they're doing, how they're exploiting the women of the church."[85] Sonia's outrage at men's misuse of women was palpable. For her, there was no other choice than to do what she did: "It seems to me that if you had seen what I had seen happening, if you had seen your leaders telling people to lie . . . and you cared about the Mormon Church, and you cared about it keeping the spirit of the Lord, what would you have done?"[86] Sonia herself, though, had no regrets. In January 1981, just over a year after her excommunication, when asked if she ever felt any self-doubt about her actions, Sonia declared to Tom Brokaw on the *Today* show, "I'd do it again, only faster and louder, I think."[87] As of my conversations with Sonia in 2022 and 2023, her rage is still palpable.

Conclusion

Sonia Johnson was completely and forever transformed by her experiences with church leaders, and those experiences had profound effects on her feminist thought as it developed over the course of her life. Her experiences with men, especially with LDS church leaders, seem to have established the frame through which she came to see the world, shaping her conviction that the problem of patriarchy *is* a problem with men, not a problem of socialization or social structure. As Mormon studies scholar Taylor G. Petrey has most recently shown, Mormonism has also long been committed to fixed, essential differences between genders.[88] Sonia carried this vision of gender difference, though in much different terms, into her later feminist thought. Over time, she became increasingly convinced that women and men are fundamentally opposites: women create, men destroy; women connect, men separate; women love, men hate. For her, men *are* the problem, and women *are* the solution.

Sonia's experiences watching male church leaders manipulate LDS women may have also shaped her conviction that all women have deeply internalized patriarchy, often so much that they take its very form against their own natures. For her, it is all women's most important lifework to unchain themselves from men's rule, to go out of their patriarchal minds. When they do, Sonia believes, they will also see her vision of a female world. Sonia's most important feminist claim is a mystical one articulated in her last book written in 2010, that "once all things were female, and they will be again."[89] Sonia believes men, and thus patriarchy, are eschatologically destined to die away and a women's paradise will emerge. She believes (hopes?) she will live to see it.

Sonia's experiences with the church also left quite a legacy for LDS feminism and politics. She mobilized important public criticisms of the church's role in politics, especially around issues regarding women, gender, and power. She was the first to mobilize a press-savvy, public, and civil disobedient opposition to attempt to affect church policies, forms of activism that were, especially in LDS terms, quite confrontational. Her confrontational style introduced church members to new avenues of expressing discontent with church leadership, albeit risky ones. Recently, in the wake of the church's vigorous campaign in 2008 on behalf of Proposition 8 in California, which banned same-sex marriages in the state until overturned by the Supreme Court, many church members turned to the same kinds of public activism Sonia had used, gathering at LDS temples in Salt Lake City, New York City, Los Angeles, and other locations.[90] In 2014, LDS feminist Kate Kelly, co-organizer of Ordain Women, which invited church leaders to consider female ordination to the priesthood, led two public protests at the semiannual General Conference all-male priesthood session. Hundreds of women gathered on Temple Square to demonstrate and publicly asked for admission to the male-only meeting.[91] At one of those protests, over four hundred of the more than five hundred attendees held proxy cards on behalf of women who were unable to attend the protest. When the church announced its 2015 policy that participating in a same-sex marriage was an excommunicable offense and that children raised in such unions could not be baptized in the church, around fifteen hundred members again gathered in protest near the church office building.[92] Once more in 2018, around eight hundred members marched on church buildings in Salt Lake City in support of former LDS bishop Sam Young, who challenged the church's policy of conducting sexually explicit interviews with its youth.[93] Two hundred others protested during Young's excommunication trial.[94]

At the same time, Sonia's excommunication was a kind of prelude to, and perhaps a blueprint for, other church discipline that has played a significant role in church and social censure against feminist and progressive ideas. We have no way of knowing how many low-profile feminists have been excommunicated for feminist or progressive critiques because the church does not make public its excommunication records. However, according to historian Joanna Brooks, Sonia's excommunication "has set up every generation of Mormon feminists since. It established this groove in the Mormon imagination that to be a feminist is to be eventually excommunicated, and it's been reinforced by the excommunication of feminist intellectuals in the fall of 1993, and it's been reinforced by firings of various BYU feminist professors, the excommunication of Ordain Women leader Kate Kelly, and on and on."[95] One recent casualty of this trend, Kate Kelly, made national headlines when she was excommunicated in 2014, by sheer happenstance in the same church building in the same stake as Sonia. In the wake of Kelly's excommunication, she interviewed Sonia, now in her eighties, for Salt Lake City's alternative radio station KRCL. Writers in the "bloggernacle" (a term often used to describe hundreds of Mormon-oriented blogs in which Mormon feminists have flourished) who have reflected on Kelly's situation almost invariably hearken back to Sonia's. Also recently excommunicated for publicly challenging elements of church doctrine or practice have been Mormon podcaster John Dehlin in 2015, aforementioned Sam Young in 2018, and LGBTQ-friendly sex therapist Natasha Helfer in 2021.[96] Clearly, the church still contains and curtails the ideas of its membership through the threat of church discipline. Moreover, whereas these members were excommunicated by force, others have asked to have their names removed from church records. An untold number of still others have simply drifted away from the church.[97]

Most impactful, though, were the questions Sonia raised about the power, agency, and status of women in the church. Although she was not the first to raise these questions, the national attention given made her the most public. Sonia once told an interviewer, "I couldn't be a feminist *and* a Mormon. I chose feminism."[98] This same devil's choice has presented itself to many feminists, often under the long shadow of Sonia's excommunication. Sonia's conflict with the church set the stage for Mormonism's understanding of feminism and the ways LDS feminists have come to engage their feminism with LDS culture and the institutional church. Linda Sillitoe claimed in 1990 that "Sonia Johnson didn't break the rules in the Church Handbook so much as the unspoken taboos. She wasn't nice. She did not conform. She didn't obey. She laundered the church's dirty linen in public."[99] Because of Sonia, in the words of one contemporary blogger, "more women became emboldened to explore other issues surrounding women's rights, including feminine theology, questioning how religious leaders handle sexual abuse cases, ecclesiastical abuse, and patriarchal scripts."[100] That is, Sonia created space for LDS feminism.

On the other hand, LDS feminism has been contained and contorted by the legacy of Sonia's excommunication and those that followed. Sonia's experience has tempered LDS feminists' willingness to critique church leaders or, for that matter, to even come out of the bloggernacle in which they have thrived. In LDS communities, the threat of church discipline, alongside a cultural commitment to conflict avoidance, constrains LDS feminism and limits the forms it takes. LDS feminists are frequently advised, sometimes even by other LDS feminists, that the way to make change in the church is through discreet diplomacy. Do not make waves, keep quiet in public and work behind the scenes, and whatever else, do not embarrass the brethren. That is, do not be like Sonia Johnson. Nonetheless, some LDS feminists have followed in her footsteps, publicly challenging leaders to create more space for women's full and equal participation in church affairs. Most of those who have done so have paid for it in some way, a few with their church membership and many at other perhaps more personal costs.

Perhaps the most somber legacy of Sonia's confrontation with the church is one of tremendous pain among LDS feminists inside and outside of the institutional church. Excommunications of feminists since Sonia have ripped the bandages from the wounds of many believers, exposing the raw, painful tissue underneath. I have been researching Sonia's life and work for about five years now and had several conversations with church members, ex-Mormons, and nonbelievers who lived through these times. Almost to a person, responses are pained and visceral. For many, the distress is still palpable and raw. Even over forty years later, there is little space within LDS culture for measured conversations about Sonia's excommunication. The legacy of her experience reminds all of us that the challenges, problems, and anguish she articulated have not been resolved.

Bibliographic Essay

Neither Sonia's thought nor her influence on Mormonism lend themselves to a traditional bibliographic essay. Sonia's contribution to Mormon thought is contained as much in the ideas developed through her public speaking and activism as it is in her published work. Her feminism during the period under discussion in this book resulted in only one publication that is easily accessible to the general public: her memoir, *From Housewife to Heretic*. However, at the time, her ideas were widely accessible through television appearances, press interviews, and speeches. Today, most of those sources are available only in archives, though a few have also been digitized. For quite some time after her excommunication, Sonia made a living as a public speaker, and many of her addresses are preserved in archives as well. Five of six of Sonia's major published works appeared well after her conflict with the LDS church, most of them barely mentioning Mormonism at all. Sonia's feminist theorizing in these monographs was primarily descriptive, tracing for readers the experiences and epiphanies that brought Sonia to her conclusions.

Calling the Church to Account

Sonia's first public appearance as the public face of Mormon feminism was in August 1978 before the Senate Judiciary Committee. In this testimony, Sonia demonstrated the compatibility of Mormonism with women's rights with the words of early church leaders, men and women, copiously using quotations from the early LDS women's newspaper, *Woman's Exponent*, published from 1872 to 1914. She condemned the language of the church leaders of her own era declaring how "exalted" women were and suggested that true exaltation was incompatible with inequality.

As Sonia became better known, she gave nearly one hundred fifty speeches for the National Organization for Women (NOW) and probably as many or more for other organizations, churches, and universities and at marches and rallies. Perhaps the most controversial of these speeches was in Kalispell in August 1979 at a meeting of the Montana chapter of NOW. It established much of the pattern Sonia would follow in most of her other speeches over the next year or so. Sonia began her exposé with brief explanation that most Mormons opposed the ERA because they followed the prophet, not out of personal or political conviction, and that LDS women's anti-ERA activism was centrally directed by church leaders in Salt Lake City and organized by local male authorities. She claimed that the church had entered the political arena, so it can and must be lobbied and treated like a political enemy, not a church. She also discussed the funding model of LDS anti-ERA activism by which church leaders asked individuals to donate to organizations that church leaders had set up to oppose the ERA. It was in the context of the question-and-answer session following this speech in Kalispell that Sonia made her controversial statement about the missionary program, one of the misquoted statements used as evidence against her in her trial. Existing speeches indicate that Sonia reiterated many of these same themes in most of her public speeches until the defeat of the ERA in June 1982.[1]

The most intemperate and most unique speech of Sonia's early career came a month after Kalispell at the APA conference in New York City. In it, she called the church "the last unmitigated Western patriarchy" and accused it of indoctrinating its members into unconditional obedience to a prophet they believed to be infallible. Sonia claimed that especially over the decade preceding the speech, the church had systematically indoctrinated women to remain housebound and dependent on men and disempowered Relief Society women from controlling their own budget, programs, and publications. This made LDS women "bootlickers and toadies to the men of the church and destroying what little freedom of choice we had." She added that the vehemence with which church authorities attacked the ERA demonstrated their "raw panic at the idea that women might step forward as goddesses-in-the-making with [real] power."[2]

Bibliographic Essay

About a month after the APA speech, Sonia gave a third troublemaking and unique address at the Utah Women's Conference called "Off Our Pedestals, or the Chronicles of the Uppity Sisters." In it, she critiqued all societies that put women on pedestals, declaring that the metaphor reveals Western society's "savage misogyny." The context makes clear that Sonia had used the phrase "savage misogyny" to refer to all of Western patriarchy, not LDS patriarchy specifically, as the press had stated. She then read segments from letters written to her by LDS women in which they spoke back to patriarchy.

A few weeks after Sonia's excommunication, the Sunday issue of the *Washington Post* featured an essay she wrote called "Even Institutions Reap What They Sow." The essay was her most publicly available initial response to her excommunication. In it, she argued that her excommunication was but a symptom of a larger "serious moral crisis" in the church provoked by its entrance into the political arena. She believed that "the church's covert and less-than-strictly-ethical political activities may be a compromise with integrity that it simply cannot afford. Even institutions reap what they sow." Sonia reiterated this theme in speech after speech that one of these less-than-ethical activities was instructing LDS women activists to claim they acted only as private citizens and not as church representatives when their activism actually was "directed by religious leaders in Utah and, for the most part, not by their own independent informed convictions." Another was telling women "not to divulge that they had been organized by men" when Sonia believed (and the historical record seems to show) that the directive to organize came from the Special Affairs Committee and was carried out through the male priesthood hierarchies of the church. For Sonia, the men were directing the women to lie, and "requiring members to be less than honest . . . must eventually be lethal to a religious body." The article then went on to demonstrate the church's third less-than-ethical activity: "distorting evidence in order to rid itself of political opposition" in excommunicating Sonia.[3]

In 1981 and early 1982, Sonia gave two published interviews available in very different sources with very different audiences. The first of these appeared in the summer 1981 issue of *Dialogue: A Journal of Mormon Thought*, alongside a timeline of events. In this interview with Mary L. Bradford, Sonia updated primarily LDS readers on her feelings about the church since her excommunication, her bishop, Jeffrey Willis, who excommunicated her, ERA politics, and feminism within the church. Sonia told

88

Bradford, "God would never expect people who are total non-experts on this subject to give advice to experts. Women are the experts on being women, but we are told who we are and what we are and what we must feel by men who haven't a clue. . . . How can they tell me when I am feeling fulfilled?"[4] By the time of this interview, Sonia had become comfortable critiquing church leaders' religious teachings. When asked if she would ever return to the church if it changed its perspective on the ERA, she told Bradford, "They would have to change their minds on too many other things. Half the apostles would have to become women. Women would have to be called to decision-making bodies."[5] Sonia did not want her children, or anyone else, to be part of any organization in which "only *men* can make decisions." She said, "You can call it having a different role. In the end, the message is that women are not worthy."[6] Nonetheless, Sonia said, Mormon women were beginning to resist their powerlessness in the church: "I think we are coming to the point where women aren't going to let men do that anymore."[7] Sonia indicated in this interview that although she still cared deeply about her LDS sisters, she had ceased to care about the church.

In the spring of 1982, the journal *Feminist Studies* published a very different interview with Sonia by Karen Langlois. In this interview, Sonia offered a working definition of feminism that would remain fairly consistent throughout the rest of her life: "a person becomes female oriented and identifies with women instead of men."[8] After giving Langlois and readers a summary of her feminist awaking, activism, and excommunication, Sonia confirmed her single-minded commitment to the ERA. She told Langlois, "I haven't looked much beyond ratification. I am very single-issue[-oriented], and my whole being is bent on ratification of the Equal Rights Amendment. I think about it day and night. It's practically all that I think about."[9] When asked if she had any regrets, Sonia concluded the interview by saying, "I did the only thing my conscience would allow right from the start. I did what I had to do. It had to be done."[10]

It was perhaps this single-mindedness that shaped Sonia's commitment to civil disobedience during the months after her excommunication. As she recounted in many of her later speeches, a man once asked Sonia after a speech if she was "obsessed" with the ERA. Her resulting epiphany convinced Sonia that women's impulse to appear temperate, moderate, and polite was a misguided concession to patriarchy. She articulated this realization most completely in February 1981 in an article she had titled

"In Defense of Immoderation." Ironically, the publisher, *Common Cause* magazine, retitled the article from Sonia's original title to "In Defense of Equal Rights."[11] In this essay and in speeches after it, Sonia argued that civil disobedience has been central to all successful social movements, and feminists must embrace it. Sonia rejected some feminists' concerns about losing credibility with men, stating frankly that women never had credibility in the first place. She pointed out that men who make significant sacrifices for their rights, like America's founding fathers, are considered heroes. "Patrick Henry's fervent Give Me Liberty or Give Me Death gives us the delicious shivers, precisely because it is not a balanced, moderate statement. But women who do and speak as Henry did are considered immoderate and obsessed; they have gone too far." This was because under patriarchy, "women are the ones who DO the sacrificing, . . . not the ones others sacrifice FOR." Women must learn from men like America's founding fathers that "to gain ANYTHING we must be willing to risk EVERYTHING." She claimed, "The only appropriate feeling for women in the United States today is rage and the only appropriate action is immoderation."[12] By early 1981, immoderate civil disobedience and direct action had come to the center of Sonia's feminism, and by the defeat of the ERA in June 1982, Sonia had organized or participated in around eighteen major direct actions of civil disobedience for the ERA, many of which were covered in mainstream press. Even more were covered in feminist publications.[13]

Sonia's presence lent publicity to any act of civil disobedience, but two of these actions got much more attention than others. First, in October 1980, the day temple dedication ceremonies were to begin for a newly constructed LDS temple in Bellevue, Washington, just outside of Seattle, Sonia and twenty other women and one man chained themselves to the entrance gates. A banner read, "Every woman is chained by the Mormon Church."[14] During this protest, one woman, Marty LaBrosse, was pushed to the ground by a temple official and pressed charges, a series of events that received broad press coverage.[15] Second, Sonia's participation in the ERA fast in Illinois that preceded the amendment's defeat was more personally significant to her. A press release the seven fasters wrote together said the fast was to "make visible women's deprivation and witness to women's deep hunger for justice."[16] A banner appeared behind the fasters that read, "Women Hunger for Justice." After the fast, Sonia told a reporter of the epiphany she experienced during the fast: "We know that men are never going to represent us in the legislatures of this country. That is like asking the slaveholders to represent the slaves."[17] This insight would come to define Sonia's thought for the rest of her life.

Sonia's most well-known publication, published in November 1981, *From Housewife to Heretic*, appeared ninth on the *New York Times* best-selling nonfiction list in December 1981, only one month after its publication.[18] The book was reprinted in 1983 by Anchor Books and again in 1989 by Sonia's self-publishing company, Wildfire Books. Anecdotally, the 1989 edition is the most available in libraries and online and brick-and-mortar used bookstores. The book chronicles Sonia's life from when she met Rick in 1958 until the summer of 1981, when she found herself at the "end of my tolerance of a number of things. The stifling, power-hungry male-ness of the Mormon establishment," of grieving "for something which I slowly began to understand had never really existed except in my own mind."[19] The book details Sonia's experience of the series of epiphanies that initially led her to feminism, her opposition to the church and its members' anti-ERA activism, the confrontations with the church that led to her excommunication, and the many betrayals she experienced at the hands of male church leaders and the man she loved. Woven throughout these experiences are short segments of feminist insight that use Sonia's experiences to illustrate her many feminist epiphanies. The latter two-thirds of the book details more completely Sonia's version of the complex narrative of her excommunication I discussed in chapter 2. These chapters leave the reader with the distinct sense that if the deck was not stacked against Sonia from the beginning, the process was spectacularly unfair at best and it was unscrupulous and deceitful at worst.

Visioning Women's World

In 1984, Sonia ran for president of the United States. Her platform showed her commitment to feminism, "the most inclusive, the most descriptive, the most all-encompassing analysis of the human situation. It's a total world view . . . and it's the only innovative one."[20] She often repeated in campaign speeches and interviews that "the oppression of women is the archetypal oppression upon which all other oppressions—imperialism, colonialism, war—are modeled."[21] Her agenda included demilitarization, economic justice, and environmental protection, and she argued that violence against women, the human species, and the earth was of the same "conquistador" or "rapist" mind. Sonia's campaign materials declared that "I'm running to win. Because in a campaign such as ours, winning does not only mean occupancy of the Oval Office. It means many things."[22] For Sonia, it meant the opportunity to introduce radical feminist ideas into national politics, to raise consciousness, to give her supporters someone they could vote for in good conscience, and to place a woman's name on the ballot when the two major parties were "still slamming Old Boys' clubhouse door shut in women's faces."[23]

In October, just weeks before the election and the day before the first televised presidential debate, Sonia wrote a guest column in *USA Today* titled "Want a Real Debate? Invite Me." She argued that barring her from the televised debates not only violated the First Amendment but also that "democracy depends upon free and fair competition for all candidates, including their ideas. What finally compelled me to request inclusion in the debates was the realization that the two better-known candidates would neither raise nor discuss ideas upon which life on this planet depends." Sonia's article challenged the network broadcasters who had excluded her to "surprise the general public with thought-provoking, robust, irreverent, genuine debate. Invite me!"[24] The article accompanied a lawsuit Sonia and her running mate, Richard Walton, filed against television networks, trying to get into the televised debates.[25] They lost.

Sonia's second book, *Going Out of Our Minds: The Metaphysics of Liberation*, published in 1987, introduced a new style of writing and theorizing for Sonia. The book details the conclusions she came to during her ERA civil disobedience, her run for president of NOW, and her U.S. presidential campaign. Stylistically, the book unfolds as a series of epiphanies, some large and some small, that characterized the development of her ideas. The book attempts to follow function with form, written in ways that exhibit Sonia's commitment to nonhierarchical modes of doing and being. The central epiphany the book articulates is that the very nonviolent civil disobedience she had earlier advocated simply locked feminists into relationship with patriarchy, strengthening its power over women. "What we resist persists."[26] Engagement with patriarchy, even in resistance, she claims, was a powerless position because it "reinforces men's unconscious conviction that they are god Himself, or, at the very least, god's trusted stewards."[27] Sonia now believed that the central purpose of civil disobedience was not to enact political change but rather to build courage in women. Instead, Sonia began to explore in this book what a truly "women's culture" might be like.[28] For her, this meant exploring nonhierarchical and anti-institutional ways of being. As she framed it, feminists needed to stop working against what they did not want and start enacting what they did want.[29] For Sonia, women's culture needed neither formal institutions nor hierarchical leadership and instead would run on the "womanly" values of consensus, equality, and cooperation. This book describes the women's "visioning" events Sonia organized to try to "completely redesign and replant our psychic gardens" in nonpatriarchal ways.[30]

Partly on principle, Sonia did not spend much time thinking about men or men's interests. In *Going Out of Our Minds*, she did devote a chapter to "Telling the Truth" (also printed in pamphlet form in 1987). In it, she tells readers that "telling the truth is the only redemptive act of love left between the sexes."[31] Sonia argues that rape and other forms of violence against women are the primary institution of patriarchy. For Sonia, not all men rape, but it is always men who rape, and all men benefit from rape while all women are enslaved by it.[32] For Sonia, men are not the enemy because feminism, by its very nature, "has no place for the concept of 'enemy.'" Nonetheless, "telling the truth is not blaming. It's telling the truth."[33]

The book argues that to discover and embrace their true, nonpatriarchal womanliness, women must go "out of our limited, lightless, dying patriarchal minds and reach for our lives—for *all* life—deep into the cosmos that is our own souls."[34] As of this writing, a recording of one of the speeches following the publication of *Going Out of Our Minds*, titled "Going Farther Out of Our Minds," is available in two parts on YouTube.[35] The speech articulates most of the major themes of Sonia's second book.

Sonia remained a powerful but much less public figure in feminism well into the 1990s. Her four self-published books were widely read in feminist communities and reviewed in feminist journals and magazines. These publications were framed by three fundamental ideas, each book analyzing different elements of these ideas as her thought developed. First, Sonia posited women and men as distinct classes of people; all women were similar in nature and in fundamental opposition to all men, who were also similar in nature. She posited a "male" culture in which all men participated, though to varying degrees, and a "female" culture in which all women participated to the extent that they had escaped a patriarchal mindset. For

Sonia, all men work together to oppress all women. Some men also oppress other men, but in patriarchy, those men are bought off by their ability to oppress women. Women, on the other hand, are fractured and kept from connecting with each other by both their forced loyalty to patriarchy and by divisions of race, class, and sexuality, categories she believes patriarchy invented to separate women from one another.

Second, Sonia was deeply influenced by feminist theorist Mary Daly's concept of patriarchal reversal. Briefly, Daly defines patriarchal reversal as men either displacing their own vices onto women or claiming women's virtues or ideas as their own (often while claiming to raise women's status and affirm their dignity). One example of the first reversal is the claim that feminists are anti-male. This reversal displaces male malice onto women, "implying that women are the initiators of enmity, blaming the victims for The War [sic]" they did not create.[36] Daly develops the second reversal most thoroughly in relationship to the emergence of Christian theology in place of ancient goddess-based religions. Christianity claimed for men the generative power belonging to women by positing a male creator and his creation, Adam, who then gave birth via his rib to Eve. Sonia extended Daly's conception of patriarchal reversal to claim not just that men reverse engineer gendered virtue and vice but that all patriarchal ideas by their very nature tell the opposite of the truth. Over time, the concept increasingly became a kind of barometer of veracity, a principle by which Sonia measured the truth of her own and others' feminist ideas. The more opposite patriarchy an idea was, the more correct it must be.

Third, Sonia believed that patriarchy's deepest and most intractable wound was that it brainwashed women to hate themselves and each other. For her, the most transgressive and transformative feminist act was self-actualization and self-love. Women's alliances with and love and concern for men was the greatest of all patriarchal reversals, convincing women that men matter more when, in fact, women do because they "have the saving gift to give earth's people, the only alternative to the male model that imperils us all."[37] For Sonia, self-actualization was the only way to shuck off women's internalization of patriarchy and emerge as true selves. Self-love also inevitably led to the love of other women.

By the time Sonia published her third book, *Wildfire* (1989), she had come to believe that women must disengage completely from patriarchy and from men. *Wildfire* articulates more fully what a women's world might look like and, more important, how to enact it. In the book, Sonia gives readers an existential and anarchist feminism, calling women into responsibility and advocating radical feminist freedom and self-government. Women must divorce themselves from the government of the patriarchal nation-state and its accompanying dualistic ideas of justice and equality ("Just/Us and Hequality"), concepts that imply hierarchy and comparison, punishment and reward. Sonia believed that although women might begin in communities of women living together, creating their own rules in nonhierarchical, biophilic, life-affirming, and loving ways, their ability to create these worlds on larger scales was limited by their patriarchal programming. Women, Sonia argues, must begin to "live *as if* we are free, *as if* we were in every way the women we have dreamed of becoming, *as if* the world was what we want it to be."[38] Women must dispense with the patriarchal notion that a "living" must be "earned" and instead embrace the interconnectedness of all things and give and receive freely in a community where masculine notions of value (in the monetary sense) have been replaced with womanly values of gift giving. Living this way, she believed, would bring a new world into being. For her, this is the great work of women—to create the world anew.

Sonia's difficult lesbian relationships and breakups brought her to radical conclusions about the nature of relationships, sex, and intimacy, which she discusses in her fourth book, *The Ship that Sailed into the Living Room*, published in 1991. Here, she argues that the concept and practice of sexuality and sex was always already infected with patriarchy. Sex, couple-hood, and love, even between women, had been institutionalized and commodified by patriarchy, integrated into an economy of hierarchical sadomasochistic exchange. Relationships tie their participants to presumptions and expectations neither participant wants, creating a "closed system" rooted in sexual exclusivity.[39] As sex becomes the defining feature of the relationship, sex becomes patriarchal because of its goal orientation, one partner eliciting and controlling the sexual responses of the other. Romantic and sexual coupledom (or "couple-dumb" as she called it) inevitably creates expectations, demands, and stimulus-response patterns that distances participants from their true selves and creates power imbalances between partners. Two, she argues, was "the perfect number for coercion."[40] The attending commitment of intimate partnerships, Sonia argues, required that one be false to oneself to be "true" to another. At the end of the book, Sonia discusses how she began to explore ways of touching intimately without wanting something from it, only for the touch itself, and committing not to another but to the self. She calls for a world in which women touch without regard to any end except the pleasure of touching. This, she at once claimed and hoped, would return women to their intrinsic power, giving themselves and each other all the intimacy they can bear but none of the sex that oppressed them.

Sonia's fifth book, *Out of This World*, which she wrote with Jade DeForest and published in 1993, appears to be a kind of sequel to both *Wildfire* and *The Ship that Sailed into the Living Room*. In Sonia's conversations with me in September 2022, she reported that an original unpublished manuscript had been an autobiographical account of how and why the Wildfire community in New Mexico had fallen apart. A publisher friend of hers worried that community members might sue Sonia for revelations in the book, so Sonia and DeForest burned that draft and rewrote the book as a "fictional-ized true-life" story containing very little analysis of the trials and troubles of the community.[41] In the published book, Sonia and Jean (an alias for Jade) and their compatriots trace their journey toward enacting women's world. What is most significant about the work is the ways Sonia and Jean work together to dismantle any smidgeon of hierarchy or control between them as they and their companions arrive at "the beginning of women's world, a world of love, joy, contentment, peace, and abundance. A world free of sadomasochism, of competition, of jealousy, anger and hatred. A world where all living things exist harmoniously and in balance because there is no maleness to cause turmoil and suffering. A world elegantly and exquisitely simple and pure."[42] For Sonia, this world by its very nature could only exist among women.

Sonia developed her most complete feminist vision when she published her last book, *The SisterWitch Conspiracy*, in 2010. In it, she aimed "to remember femaleness, to invent it where memory fails, to delight in my passion for the lost world that is its essence."[43] She develops her most important claim told to Jade by a Native geneticist and to Sonia by a woman who had visited Indigenous women in Australia: the mystical vision that "once all things were female." The book traces a "forgotten" history of women's tragic exit from their world, giving readers what amounts to a theology steeped in gender essentialism and a prophetic application of the astronomical theory of the big bang. Before the big bang, Sonia believes, time did not exist and everything that existed was female in total intimacy and timeless oneness. The big bang introduced maleness and with it time, separation, and physical limitations into the universe. Accompanying this cosmology is an esoteric interpretation of some genetic ideas from 2004 through which Sonia conceives of maleness as a genetic mutation that is, by its very nature, opposite the life-creating and loving energy of women.[44] She claims that patriarchy "is what they [men] *are*, their natural and ineluctable mode of existence. . . . Patriarchy is a revelation to us of men's most hidden inner selves," of men's violence, rapaciousness, obsession with killing.[45] Asking men to be or behave other than their genetic nature is futile.

In this book, Sonia claims that over the course of human history, men only survived because women ensured and continue to ensure men's survival by sacrificing their own energy and resources on men's behalf. Over time, men increasingly exploited women's sacrifice, unleashed their rapaciousness on all that was, including the women who saved men from themselves and from each other. All the while, women forgot their now-elapsed and increasingly forbidden world while men replaced it with their own patriarchal rule. However, Sonia also writes that maleness, and with it patriarchy, is genetically destined to die out, and women must do all they can to survive the time between now and the death of maleness to bring women's world back into existence. Sonia concludes her final work by renewing her covenant with all women to do whatever is necessary to outlast maleness and reunite in total intimacy and timeless femaleness with all things. She ends the book by telling her woman readers that "until then, and forever after, my dearest loves, you have my heart and my life."[46]

Notes

Chapter 1. "Patriarchy Is a Sham"

1. Because family names mark patrifocal lineage and patriarchal authority and because "Johnson" is frequently used as a slang for male genitalia, Sonia requested in conversation with me on May 24, 2022, that I use her first name throughout the book.

2. See, for example, Roy Gibson, "No Such Thing as a Free Lunch," *Utah Holiday*, February 1980, and an untitled, undated document in Box 7, Folder 3, Beverly Campbell Papers, 1960–2013, Church History Library, the Church of Jesus Christ of Latter-day Saints, Salt Lake City. Library cited hereafter as CHL.

3. Sonia Johnson, 430–2650, n.d., Item 17, Sonia Johnson Audio-Visual Collection, 1976–1981, J. Willard Marriott Library, Special Collections, University of Utah. Collection cited hereafter as SJAV.

4. Johnson, 430–2650.

5. Sonia Johnson in discussion with the author, May 23, 2023.

6. Sonia Johnson, *From Housewife to Heretic: One Woman's Spiritual Awakening and Her Excommunication from the Mormon Church* (Albuquerque: Wildfire Books, 1989), 62.

7. Johnson, *From Housewife to Heretic*, 63–65.

8. Johnson, *From Housewife to Heretic*, 74.

9. In discussion with the author, January 22, 2023.

10. Johnson, *From Housewife to Heretic*, 77–78, quoted material on 77.

11. Johnson, *From Housewife to Heretic*, 25.

12. For a biography of Eugene England, see Kristine Haglund, *Eugene England: A Mormon Liberal* (Urbana: University of Illinois Press, 2021).

13. See "News of the Church," *Ensign*, August 1975, accessed June 20, 2020, https://abn.churchofjesuschrist.org/study/ensign/1975/08/news-of-the-church/new-information-on-church-policies?lang=eng.

14. Johnson, *From Housewife to Heretic*, 85; italics in original.

15. To Sonia Johnson from Gwen F. Johnson, April 16, 1980, Item 18, SJAV. Side B of this recording is Sonia Johnson reflecting on her life.

16. Johnson, 430–2650.

17. To Sonia, Side B.

18. Johnson, *From Housewife to Heretic*, 44–46.

19. To Sonia, Side B.

20. Johnson, *From Housewife to Heretic*, 55.

21. Susan D. Becker, *The Origins of the Equal Rights Amendment: American Feminism between the Wars* (Westport, CT: Greenwood, 1981); Mary Frances Berry, *Why ERA Failed: Politics, Women's Rights, and the Amending Process of the Constitution* (Bloomington: Indiana University Press, 1986); Martha Sontag Bradley, *Pedestals and Podiums: Utah Women, Religious Authority, and Equal Rights* (Salt Lake City: Signature Books, 2005); Rebecca DeWolf, *Gendered Citizenship: The Original Conflict over the Equal Rights Amendment, 1920–1963* (Lincoln: University of Nebraska Press, 2021); Jane J. Mansbridge, *Why We Lost the ERA* (Chicago: University of Chicago Press, 1986); Donald G. Mathews and Jane Sherron De Hart, *Sex, Gender, and the Politics of ERA: A State and the Nation* (New York: Oxford University Press, 1990).

22. See Laurel Thatcher Ulrich, "Mormon Women in the History of Second-Wave Feminism," *Dialogue: A Journal of Mormon Thought* 43, no. 2 (Summer 2010): 45–63.

23. Claudia L. Bushman, "*Exponent II* Is Born," *Exponent II*, July 1974, 2.

24. Nancy Tate Dredge, "Key Turning Points in *Exponent II*'s History," *Dialogue: A Journal of Mormon Thought* 29, no. 2 (Summer 2016): 136.

25. Jan Shipps, "*Exponent II*: Mormonism's Stealth Alternative," *Exponent II* 22 (Summer 1999): 28–33.

26. Bradley, *Pedestals and Podiums*, 134. See also Martha Sonntag Bradley, "The Relief Society and the International Women's Year," *Journal of Mormon History* 21, no. 1 (Spring 1995): 106–67, https://www.jstor.org/stable/23286500; and D. Michael Quinn, "A National Force, 1970s–1990s," in *The Mormon Hierarchy: Extensions of Power* (Salt Lake City: Signature Books, 1997).

27. Dear Sonia, n.d., Item 20, SJAV.

28. Dear Sonia.

29. Dear Sonia.

30. Sonia Johnson, Alison Cheek and Sonia Johnson at NOW and Well-Woman Program, April 14, 1980, 7, Box 24, Folder 8, Sonia Johnson Papers, 1958–1983, J. Willard Marriott Library Special Collections, University of Utah. Collection cited hereafter as SJP.

31. Johnson, *From Housewife to Heretic*, 102.

32. Focus on Salt Lake Sonia Johnson Broadcast, undated, Gerry Pond Audiovisual Files, CHL.

33. Johnson, NOW and WellWoman Program, 7. The table of contents of the January and February 1977 issues of *Pageant* magazine, the last two ever printed, show no articles transparently related to the ERA.

34. Sonia Johnson, National Women's Political Caucus Speech, Los Altos, California, n.d., Item 15, SJAV.

35. Sonia Johnson, Sonia Johnson Audiotape, 1982, Box 1, Folder 11, Mary R. Boone Papers, 1982–1983, 2006, Archival Collections at North Carolina State University Libraries, Raleigh.

36. Sonia Johnson, Housewife to Heretic [Speech], November 19, 1981, Gerry Pond Audiovisual Files, CHL. See also, Johnson, *From Housewife to Heretic*, 103–4. Sonia later claimed the article appeared in a magazine called *Coronet*. See Peggy Fletcher Stack, David Noyce, Kate Kelly, and Sonia Johnson, "Sonia Johnson and Kate Kelly Discuss Their Excommunications and Long Fight for ERA," *Mormonland* podcast, April 6, 2022, accessed September 30, 2022, https://www.sltrib.com/religion/2022/04/06/mormon-land-sonia-johnson/.

37. Johnson, *From Housewife to Heretic*, 106.

38. Johnson, *From Housewife to Heretic*, 112.

39. Transcript of the Hearing of the U.S. Senate Committee on the Judiciary, Subcommittee on the Constitution, found in Box 9, Folder 1, SJP. See also Johnson, *From Housewife to Heretic*, 135.

40. This event was covered in the press in Washington, D.C., and surrounding states. See Box 27, Folder 1, SJP.

41. See, for example, Johnson, Los Altos, and Sonia Johnson, Speech in Tri-Cities, Washington, DC, October 29, 1979, Item 3, SJAV.

42. First Presidency Statement, October 12, 1978, in "The Church and the Proposed Equal Rights Amendment: A Moral Issue," pamphlet included with the *Ensign*, March 1980, accessed June 26, 2022, https://www.churchofjesuschrist.org/study/ensign/1980/03/the-church-and-the-proposed-equal-rights-amendment-a-moral-issue?lang=eng. Cited hereafter as the Gray Book.

43. Lisa Cronin Wohl, "A Mormon Connection: The Defeat of the ERA in Nevada," *Ms.* magazine, July 1977, in Box 3, Folder 9, SJP.

44. 1978 Minutes of a Meeting of Latter-day Saint Women's Coalition, November 8, 1978, 15, CHL.

45. *Oakton Stake Newsletter*, November 1978, Box 3, Folder 7, SJP.

46. Diane Weathers, "Can a Mormon Support the ERA?" *Newsweek*, December 1979, 88, CHL.

47. Untitled newspaper clipping, *Loudoun Times-Mirror*, December 13, 1979, n.p., in an unprocessed Sonia Johnson collection, Merrill-Cazier Library, Special Collections and Archives Division, Utah State University. Library cited hereafter as USU.

48. "ERA Group to Fly Banner at Mormon Meet," *Los Angeles Times*, April 1, 1979.

49. Sonia Johnson, Camilla, Item 12, SJAV.

50. Some of these women included Jan Tyler, Kris Barrett, and Marilee Latta.

51. Martha Bayles, "Nonfiction in Brief," *New York Times*, December 13, 1981, ProQuest Historical Newspapers.

52. In 2020, the LDS church stopped using the term "excommunication" and uses "withdrawal of membership" instead. Here, I will use the term "excommunication" because it most accurately represents the historical context of Johnson's experience. See "32.11.4," *General Handbook: Serving in the Church of Jesus Christ of Latter-day Saints* (Salt Lake City: Church of Jesus Christ of Latter-day Saints, 2020).

53. Richard T. Johnson to Jeffrey Willis, December 11, 1979, Box 3 Folder 2, SJP.

54. Sonia Johnson on the LDS church, Gordon B. Hinckley and the ERA, Item 22, SJAV.

55. Johnson, Housewife to Heretic speech.

56. Peggy Fletcher Stack, "40 Years after Her Mormon Excommunication, ERA Firebrand Sonia Johnson Salutes Today's 'Wonderful' Women, Says Men 'Bore' Her," *Salt Lake Tribune*, January 18, 2019, accessed December 31, 2021, https://www.sltrib.com/religion/2019/01/18/years-after-her-mormon/.

57. Sonia Johnson at the Democratic National Convention, New York City, 1980, in "Women Speak at the Democratic Convention," Pacifica Radio Archives, North Hollywood, California. Internet archive. Retrieved December 30, 2021, https://archive.org/details/pacifica_radio_archives-AZ0487.

58. Sonia Johnson, "In Defense of Equal Rights," *Common Cause*, February 1981, News, Policy, and Politics Magazine Archive.

59. Johnson, "In Defense of Equal Rights."

60. "Protester at Mormon Temple Accuses Church of Assault, Violating Her Freedom," *Seattle Times*, April 22, 1981, found in Box 9, Folder 23, SJP. Court documents are available in Box 9, Folders 22. Additional press coverage is available in Folders 22–24.

61. Sonia Johnson, *Going Out of Our Minds: The Metaphysics of Liberation* (Berkeley: Crossing Press, 1987), 36.

62. Johnson, *Going Out of Our Minds*, 38.

63. Johnson, *Going Out of Our Minds*, 37.

64. Johnson, *Going Out of Our Minds*, 95.

65. Johnson, *Going Out of Our Minds*, 125.

66. Johnson, *Going Out of Our Minds*, 26–27, quotation on 27.

67. See Sonia Johnson, *The SisterWitch Conspiracy* (Lexington, KY: Sonia Johnson, 2010), 89–96.

68. Campaign poster, in unprocessed Sonia Johnson collection, USU.

69. Sonia Johnson—Citizen for President, Statement to the Press, October 24, 1983, Box 7, Folder 9, Mormons for ERA Collection, USU.

70. Johnson, *Going Out of Our Minds*, 192.

71. "Sonia Johnson," *Austin Perspective*, PBS, January 31, 1984, CHL.

72. Johnson, *Going Out of Our Minds*, 192, 196.

73. Sonia Johnson, *Wildfire: Igniting the She/Volution* (Albuquerque: Wildfire Books, 1989), 175.

74. Johnson, *Going Out of Our Minds*, 283–86.

75. Sonia Johnson, *The Ship that Sailed into the Living Room: Sex and Intimacy Reconsidered* (Estancia, NM: Wildfire Books, 1991), 248.

76. Transcript of Sonia Johnson interviewed by Janet Paulk, Activist Women Oral History Project, Special Collections Department and Archives, Georgia State University, Atlanta, part 2, 17.

77. Johnson, interviewed by Paulk, part 1, 87–91.

78. Johnson, interviewed by Paulk, part 1, 86–91.

79. Johnson, interviewed by Paulk, part 2, 23.

80. Johnson, interviewed by Paulk, part 2, 21.

81. Johnson, interviewed by Paulk, part 2, 25.

82. See Johnson, *SisterWitch*, 129–31.

83. Sonia Johnson, in discussion with the author, January 20, 2023.

84. See, for example, "Fall Conference Edition with Kate Kelly, Tyler Glenn, The Bee and Books," *RadioActive*, KRCL, October 4, 2015, accessed December 31, 2021, https://krcl.org/blog/radioactive-fall-conference-edition-with-kate-kelly-tyler-glenn-the-bee-books/.

85. "The Fight for Women's Rights," *We'll Meet Again, with Ann Curry*, Season 2, Episode 6, PBS, January 2018. See also Zoe Nicholson, *The Hungry Heart: A Woman's Fast for Justice*, 2nd ed. (Long Beach, CA: Lune Soleil Press, 2019).

86. See Sonia Johnson, Epilogue, in Nicholson, *The Hungry Heart*, 194–97.

87. Johnson, Epilogue, 197.

Chapter Two. "Well, I'm About to Find Out"

1. Sonia Johnson, Excommunication, December 1, 1979, A0099, Item 5, SJAV. Johnson's appearance with Diane Sawyer appears after the recording of Johnson's excommunication.

2. Linda Sillitoe, "Church Politics and Sonia Johnson: The Central Conundrum," *Sunstone* January–February 1980, 42.

3. Sonia Johnson in discussion with the author, May 23, 2022.

4. See, for example, Maxine Hanks, ed., *Women and Authority: Re-emerging Mormon Feminism* (Salt Lake City: Signature Books, 1992); and Joanna Brooks, Rachel Hunt Steenblik, and Hannah Wheelright, eds., *Mormon Feminism: Essential Writings* (New York: Oxford University Press, 2016).

5. Sillitoe, "Church Politics," 38.

6. Sonia Johnson, Interview with Patrick Greenlaw, Item 7, SJAV.

7. Barbara B. Smith, "Relief Society General President Opposes ERA," *Ensign*, February 1975, accessed September 6, 2022, https://www.churchofjesuschrist .org/study/ensign/1975/02/news-of-the-church/relief-society-general-president -opposes-era?lang=eng.

8. "Equal Rights Amendment," *Church News*, January 11, 1975.

9. "Most Favor Full Rights for Women," *Deseret News*, November 15, 1974, Deseret News Online Newspaper Archive.

10. John Unger Zussman and Shauna M. Adix, "Content and Conjecture in the Equal Rights Amendment Controversy in Utah," *Women's Studies International Forum* 5, no. 5 (1982): 478–79, https://doi-org.unco.idm.oclc.org/ 10.1016/0277-5395(82)90009-7.

11. Sillitoe, "Church Politics," 36.

12. First Presidency Statement on the ERA, October 22, 1976, in the Gray Book.

13. See, for example, Spencer W. Kimball, N. Eldon Tanner, Marion G. Romney, Ezra Taft Benson, Mark E. Petersen, LeGrand Richards, Boyd K. Packer, Marvin J. Ashton, Bruce R. McConkie, David B. Haight, Neal A. Maxwell, Marion D. Hanks, Rex D. Pinegar, G. Homer Durham, James M. Paramore, *Woman* (Salt Lake City: Deseret Book, 1979).

14. First Presidency Statement, August 26, 1978, in the Gray Book.

15. First Presidency Statement, October 12, 1978, in the Gray Book.

16. First Presidency Statement, August 26, 1978, in the Gray Book.

17. First Presidency Statement, August 26, 1978, in the Gray Book.

18. Church Presidency (Spencer W. Kimball, N. Eldon Tanner, and Marian G. Romney) to All Stake, Mission, and District Presidents, Bishops and Branch Presidents in the United States, June 29, 1979, Beverly Campbell Papers, Box 7, Folder 3, CHL. Item identified as "To be read in sacrament meetings July 1, 1979."

19. The Gray Book.

20. See, for example, the analysis of North Carolina senator Sam Ervin's objections in Mathews and De Hart, *Sex, Gender, and the Politics of ERA*, 28–53; Phyllis Schlafly, "The Effect of Equal Rights Amendments in State Constitu-

tions," *Policy Review* 9 (July 1979): 55–84; and Rex E. Lee, *A Lawyer Looks at the Equal Rights Amendment* (Provo, Utah: Brigham Young University Press, 1980). Schlafly's article was reprinted as a pamphlet and in her newsletter, *The Phyllis Schlafly Report* 13, no. 1 (August 1979), accessed September 30, 2022, https://eagleforum.org/wp-content/uploads/2017/03/PSR-Aug1979.pdf.

21. Interview with Julie Beck and Barbara Smith, n.d., Church of Jesus Christ of Latter-day Saints Media Library, Women of Conviction collection, accessed September 6, 2022, https://www.churchofjesuschrist.org/media/video/2012 -08-0001-an-interview-with-barbara-smith?lang=eng.

22. Quinn, "A National Force," 400. See also Lori Motzkus Wilkinson, "Buttons, Banners, and Pie: Mormon Women's Grassroots Movements," *Journal of Mormon History* 44, no. 4 (October 2018): 112–37, https://doi-org.unco.idm .oclc.org/10.5406/jmormhist.44.4.0112.

23. "Prophet Calls for Positive Action against ERA," *Oakton Stake Newsletter*, Autumn 1978, MS 225, MERA Papers, Box 12, Folder 13, USU.

24. Minutes, 1. For readability, I have removed capital letters presumably added by the notetakers.

25. Interview with Patrick Greenlaw and Beverly Campbell, February 3, 1980, Item 7, SJAV.

26. Minutes, 2. The first sentence is capitalized in the original.

27. Campbell's two influential books are *Eve and the Choice Made in Eden* (Salt Lake City: Bookcraft, 2002) and *Eve and the Mortal Journey: Finding Wholeness, Happiness, and Strength* (Salt Lake City: Deseret Book, 2005).

28. Minutes, 4.

29. Minutes, 12. All but the last sentence is capitalized in original.

30. Minutes 17. Capitalization in original.

31. Minutes 18. Capitalization in original.

32. For the most thorough investigation of the church's role in LDS women's ERA activism, see Quinn, "A National Force," 373–406.

33. Johnson, Tri-Cities.

34. Johnson, Speech in Fresno, California, n.d., Item 16, SJAV.

35. Johnson, Fresno.

36. Sonia Johnson Speech Excerpts Question and Answer Session at Provo Women's Cultural Hall, July 28, 1981, Gerry Pond Audiovisual Files, CHL.

37. Johnson, Camilla.

38. Cheek and Johnson at NOW.

39. Johnson Interview with Greenlaw.

40. Karen S. Langlois and Sonia Johnson, "An Interview with Sonia Johnson," *Feminist Studies* 8, no. 1 (Spring 1982): 15, https://doi-org.unco.idm.oclc.org/ 10.2307/3177577.

41. Marjorie Hyer, "Mormon Fights Off Expulsion for Now," *Washington Post*, November 18, 1979, Thomas Reuters Westlaw Campus Research.

42. Johnson, Fresno.

43. Sonia Johnson in discussion with the author, May 23, 2022.

44. Vera Glaser, "Sonia Decries LDS 'Witch Hunt,'" *Salt Lake Tribune*, November 26, 1979, https://newspapers.lib.utah.edu/ark:/87278/s6s811zr/29024689.

45. Sillitoe, "Church Politics," 39.

46. At least initially, scholarship on the ERA seems to have followed suit. The three earliest studies of the ERA hardly discuss the LDS church at all, and when they do, they only mention Sonia Johnson's excommunication. See Berry, *Why ERA Failed*; Mansbridge, *Why We Lost the ERA*; and Mathews and De Hart, *Sex, Gender, and the Politics of ERA*.

47. Jeffrey H. Willis to Sonia Johnson, November 14, 1979, Box 3, Folder 3, SJP. Because excommunications are not generally made public, we do not know if this was typical.

48. Alice Allred Pottmyer, "Sonia Johnson: Mormonism's Feminist Heretic," in *Differing Visions: Dissenters in Mormon History*, ed. Roger D. Launius and Linda Thatcher (Urbana: University of Illinois Press, 1994), 366–89.

49. Sonia Johnson on *Donahue* program and Beverly Campbell's counteract to Donahue's interview, Item 6, SJAV.

50. Johnson, Reflections on Excommunication and Divorce, Item 19, SJAV.

51. Johnson, *From Housewife to Heretic*, 289–90.

52. Johnson, *From Housewife to Heretic*, 266.

53. Johnson, *From Housewife to Heretic*, 293–96.

54. Johnson, Reflections on Excommunication and Divorce.

55. Johnson, Reflections on Excommunication and Divorce.

56. Johnson, Reflections on Excommunication and Divorce.

57. Johnson, *From Housewife to Heretic*, 300.

58. Johnson, *From Housewife to Heretic*, 306.

59. Johnson, *From Housewife to Heretic*, 307.

60. Jeffrey Willis to Sonia Johnson, November 27, 1979, Box 3 Folder 3, SJP.

61. Sonia Johnson, Appeal to Earl Roueche, n.d., Box 3, Folder 3, SJP.

62. For a discussion of what witnesses said at the trial, see Bradley, *Pedestals and Podiums*, 364–65. Johnson claims her verdict was decided before the trial in Johnson, Reflections on Excommunication and Divorce.

63. Johnson, Reflections on Excommunication and Divorce. This is a recording of various conversations and events outside the church building in Virginia during and after Sonia's December 1 excommunication trial.

64. Johnson, Excommunication.

65. Johnson, Excommunication.

66. On rumors that Johnson had been sexually immoral, see Michael J. Weiss, "Irked by Sonia Johnson's ERA Crusade, Church Elders Throw the Book of Mormon at Her," *People*, December 1979, 45, in CHL.

67. Willis to Johnson, December 5, 1979, Box 3, Folder 3, SJP.

68. "Sonia Johnson Press Release," December 5, 1979, CHL.

69. Sonia Johnson to Spencer W. Kimball, April 22, 1980, Box 3, Folder 4, SJP.

70. Beverly Little and Marty LaBrosse, interview with Sisters by Cheryl Dalton, December 12, 1980, Item 9, SJAV. After the interview, the latter part of Johnson's speech in Kalispell on August 25, 1979, appears. More extensive portions of the speech appear in Sonia Johnson, Mormons for ERA, National Organization for Women, Montana State Convention, Kalispell, Montana, Audio Only, August 25, 1979, A0099, item 2, SJAV.

71. Johnson, Fresno.

72. Weathers, "Can a Mormon Support the ERA?" 88.

73. [Linda Thielke,] "Get off Pedestal, ERA Advocate Tells LDS Women," *Deseret News*, October 27, 1979, Google Books. Linda Sillitoe and Paul Swenson report that Thielke had lost her notes from the conference, so she made this error by misremembering Johnson's speech and that the Women's Resource Center at the University of Utah had a tape recording of the speech that proved Johnson did not use the phrase "savage misogyny" to refer to the LDS church specifically. See Linda Sillitoe and Paul Swenson, "The Excommunication of Sonia Johnson: A Moral Issue," *Utah Holiday Magazine*, January 1980, 23–24.

74. Sonia Johnson, "Off Our Pedestals, or the Chronicles of the Uppity Sisters," Box 24, Folder 3, SJP, 1.

75. Johnson, "Off Our Pedestals," 1.

76. Johnson, Appeal to Roueche.

77. See, for example, N. Eldon Tanner, "The Debate Is Over," *Ensign*, August 1979, accessed June 20, 2021, https://www.churchofjesuschrist.org/study/ensign/1979/08/the-debate-is-over?lang=eng.

78. Sonia Johnson, "Patriarchal Panic: Sexual Politics in the Mormon Church," Box 24, Folder 1, SJP.

79. Johnson, "Patriarchal Panic." See also William C. Wertz, "LDS President Opposes ERA, Encourages Women to be Wives," *Rexburg Standard*, June 19, 1979.

80. Johnson, "Patriarchal Panic."

81. Johnson, "Patriarchal Panic."

82. "Excommunicated: Mormon ERA Backer to Fight On," *News-Sun*, December 6, 1979, in unprocessed Sonia Johnson collection, USU.

83. Johnson, Appeal to Roueche.

84. Johnson, Reflections on Excommunication and Divorce.

85. Johnson, Excommunication.

86. Johnson, Excommunication.

87. Johnson, Excommunication.

88. Johnson, Reflections on Excommunication and Divorce.

89. Willis to Johnson, December 5, 1979, Box 3, Folder 3, SJP.

90. Johnson, *From Housewife to Heretic*, 331.

91. See Johnson to Kimball, April 22, 1980.

92. "Sonia Johnson Press Release."

93. "Church Court Action Clarified," *Ensign*, March 1980, accessed May 21, 2021, https://abn.churchofjesuschrist.org/study/ensign/1980/03/news-of-the -church/church-court-action-clarified?lang=eng.

94. Johnson, Appeal to Roueche.

95. Johnson on *Donahue*.

96. Earl Roueche to Sonia Johnson, March 24, 1980, Box 3, Folder 3, SJP.

97. Johnson to Kimball, April 22, 1980.

98. Sonia Johnson to Spencer W. Kimball, May 28, 1980, Box 3, Folder 2, SJP.

99. "Rebuff to ERA Supporter," *Washington Post*, June 30, 1980, Thomas Reuters Westlaw Campus Research.

100. See note in Johnson, *From Housewife to Heretic*, 335.

101. Johnson on *Donahue*.

102. Langlois and Johnson, 16.

103. Jim Castelli, "Scholar Says Feminist's Church Trial Aimed at Influencing Other Mormons," *Washington Star*, December 8, 1979, Box 7, Folder 5, Beverly Campbell Papers, 1960–2013, CHL.

104. Vera Glaser, "Mormonism Swallows You Whole," *USU Digital Exhibits*, accessed January 25, 2022, http://exhibits.usu.edu/items/show/17441. Reprinted from *Miami Herald*, January 14, 1980.

105. See Neil J. Young, "'The ERA Is Moral Issue': The Mormon Church, LDS Women, and the Defeat of the Equal Rights Amendment," *American Quarterly* 59, no. 3 (September 2007), https://www.jstor.org/stable/40068443.

106. Colleen McDannell, *Sister Saints: Mormon Women since the End of Polygamy* (New York: Oxford University Press, 2019).

107. Vera Glaser, "Mormon Men Call All the Shots," *Miami Herald*, January 14, 1980, *USU Digital Exhibits*, accessed January 25, 2022, http://exhibits.usu.edu/ items/show/17442.

108. Kathleen Flake, "Bearing the Weight," *Sunstone* 13 (October 1989): 34.

109. Linda Sillitoe, "Off the Record," *Sunstone*, December 1990, 12.

110. Vera Goodman, "ERA: The New Face of Missionaries," *New Directions for Women* 10 (July/August 1981): 18, CHL.

111. Zussman and Adix, "Content and Conjecture," 482–86, quoted material on 482 and 485.

112. Quinn, "A National Force," 396.

Chapter Three. "A Compromise with Integrity that It Simply Cannot Afford"

1. Sonia Johnson, "Even Institutions Reap What They Sow," *Washington Post*, December 23, 1979.

2. Joseph Smith, "The Articles of Faith," Church of Jesus Christ of Latter-day Saints, accessed June 13, 2022, https://www.churchofjesuschrist.org/comeunto christ/article/articles-of-faith.

3. J. Spencer Fluhman, *"A Peculiar People": Anti-Mormonism and the Making of Religion in Nineteenth-Century America* (Chapel Hill: University of North Carolina Press, 2014); Benjamin E. Park, *Kingdom of Nauvoo: The Rise and Fall of a Religious Empire on the American Frontier* (New York: Liveright, 2020); Kathleen Flake, *The Politics of American Religious Identity: The Seating of Senator Reed Smoot, Mormon Apostle* (Chapel Hill: University of North Carolina Press, 2004); Christine Talbot, *A Foreign Kingdom: Mormons and Polygamy in American Political Culture, 1852–1890* (Urbana-Champaign: University of Illinois Press, 2013).

4. Fluhman, *"A Peculiar People."* Quotation from J. H. Beadle, "The Mormon Theocracy," *Scribner's Monthly* 14, no. 3 (July 1877): 391.

5. Flake, *The Politics of American Religious Identity.*

6. Armand Mauss, *The Angel and the Beehive: The Mormon Struggle with Assimilation* (Urbana-Champaign: University of Illinois Press, 1994), 78.

7. Mauss, *The Angel and the Beehive*, 88.

8. Young, "'The ERA Is a Moral Issue,'" 628. See also Quinn, "A National Force," 373–406.

9. Focus on Salt Lake Sonia Johnson broadcast.

10. Johnson, Tri-Cities.

11. Focus on Salt Lake Sonia Johnson Broadcast.

12. Idsvoog Program, Item 4, SJAV. See also Kimball et al., *Woman.*

13. Johnson, Tri-Cities.

14. Johnson, Fresno.

15. Sonia Johnson, Excommunication. This recording of Sonia's appearance on the *Today* show appears at the end of the recording.

16. Focus on Salt Lake Sonia Johnson Broadcast.

17. Johnson, Tri-Cities.

18. Focus on Salt Lake Sonia Johnson Broadcast.

19. Focus on Salt Lake Sonia Johnson Broadcast.

20. See Lester E. Bush Jr. and Armand L. Mauss, *Neither White nor Black: Mormon Scholars Encounter the Race Issue in a Universal Church* (Midvale, UT: Signature Books, 1984); Armand Mauss, *All Abraham's Children: Changing Mormon Conceptions of Race and Lineage* (Urbana: University of Illinois Press, 2003); W. Paul Reeve, *Religion of a Different Color: Race and the Mormon Struggle for Whiteness* (New York: Oxford University Press, 2015); Joanna Brooks, *Mormonism and White Supremacy: American Religion and the Problem of Racial Innocence* (New York: Oxford University Press, 2020).

21. Official Declaration 2 has appeared in every issue of the church's third book of scripture, The Doctrine and Covenants, published since 1978. Official Declaration 1 is the 1890 manifesto ending the practice of plural marriage.

22. Idsvoog Program.

23. Update on Sonia Johnson, *Extra*, 1979, KUTV News Collection, J. Willard Marriott Library Special Collections, University of Utah, Salt Lake City.

24. Johnson Interview with Greenlaw.

25. Beverly Campbell Interview, Salt Lake City, January 17, 1980, AV 4936, CHL. This interview is with David Briscoe.

26. Idsvoog Program.

27. Johnson on the LDS Church, Hinckley and the ERA.

28. Elaine Cannon, "If We Want to Go Up, We Have to Get On," *Ensign*, November 1978, accessed June 5, 2021, https://www.churchofjesuschrist.org/study/ensign/1978/11/if-we-want-to-go-up-we-have-to-get-on?lang=eng.

29. Tanner, "The Debate Is Over."

30. Quinn, "A National Force," 394.

31. Bradley, *Pedestals and Podiums*, 404.

32. O. Kendall White Jr., "Overt and Covert Policies: The Mormon Church's Anti-ERA Campaign in Virginia," *Virginia Social Science Journal* 19 (Winter 1984): 14, CHL.

33. Young, "'The ERA Is a Moral Issue,'" 624.

34. Johnson, "Patriarchal Panic."

35. Johnson, Fresno.

36. Take2, July 11, 1982, Sonia Johnson with Rod Decker, KUTV News Collection, J. Willard Marriott Special Collections, University of Utah, Salt Lake City.

37. Johnson, Fresno.

38. Take2.

39. Johnson, Tri-Cities.

40. This conclusion is borne out by Zussman and Adix, "Content and Conjecture."

41. Focus on Salt Lake Sonia Johnson Broadcast.

42. Focus on Salt Lake Sonia Johnson Broadcast.

43. Campbell Interview with Briscoe.

44. Johnson, "Even Institutions."

45. Johnson, Tri-Cities.

46. The Gray Book.

47. "Contact: The ERA, Right or Wrong for the Mormon Woman?" January 13, 1980, Donahue, Contact, Other, MS 24650, CHL.

48. Mary Lou Nolan, "Mormon Debate on ERA Focuses on Missouri Action," *Kansas City Star*, January 10, 1980, in Box 4, Folder 17, Beverly Campbell Papers, CHL.

49. See Schlafly, "The Effect of the Equal Rights Amendment," 55–84; Lee, *A Lawyer Looks*; and Paul A. Freund, "The Equal Rights Amendment Is Not the Way," *Harvard Civil Rights—Civil Liberties Law Review* 6, no. 2 (March 1971): 234–42, HeinOnline Law Journal Library.

50. For a more thorough analysis of Campbell's misrepresentation of the legislative intent and judicial history of the ERA, see Christine Talbot, "Beverly Campbell and the ERA: Promoting Gender Anxieties on Behalf of the Brethren" (paper presented at the Mormon History Association conference, online, June 2021).

51. Paul Swenson Interview with Beverly Campbell SLC, January 17, 1980, CHL. During the Swenson interview, a bystander interrupts to address the man and addresses him as "Don." The voice sounds like LeFevre's in the church's Sonia Johnson Press Release.

52. Campbell Interview with Briscoe.

53. "Contact: The ERA."

54. Interview with Patrick Greenlaw and Beverly Campbell, February 3, 1980, Item 7, SJAV.

55. Fluhman, *"A Peculiar People,"* 7.

56. Minutes, 12. All but the last sentence is capitalized in the original.

57. Take2.

58. Jessica Savage [Savitch] Report on Sonia Johnson, undated, Gerry Pond Audiovisual Files, CHL.

59. Johnson Interview with Greenlaw.

60. Johnson, Fresno.

61. Jessica Savage [Savitch] Report.

62. Johnson, "Even Institutions."

63. Johnson, Fresno.

64. See, for example, Housewife to Heretic Speech.

65. Johnson, Tri-Cities.

66. Sillitoe and Swenson, "The Excommunication of Sonia Johnson," 22.

67. Johnson, "Even Institutions."

68. Johnson, "Even Institutions."

69. Campbell on KWMS, February 5, 1980, Gerry Pond Audiovisual Files, CHL.

70. Campbell on KWMS.

71. Johnson on *Donahue* program and Campbell's counteract. This recording is after a recording of Johnson's interview with Phil Donahue and is an interview with Beverly Campbell and Roy Gibson of KTVX News.

72. Campbell on KWMS.

73. Campbell on KWMS.

74. Campbell on KWMS.

75. Beverly Campbell ERA undated, Gerry Pond Audiovisual Files, CHL.

76. Campbell Interview with Greenlaw.

77. Zussman and Adix, "Content and Conjecture," 81.

Chapter Four. "The Grossest Misuses of Women's Religious Convictions"

1. Johnson, Kalispell.

2. Johnson, Kalispell. The records of the SAC, held at the LDS Church History Library, are closed for research, so there is no way of checking the accuracy of this claim.

3. Linda Sillitoe, notes of interview with regional representative Donald Ladd, February 15, 1979, Box 5, Folder 10, Collection of Utah Women's Issues, J. Willard Marriott Library Special Collections, University of Utah, Salt Lake City.

4. Sillitoe and Swenson, "The Excommunication of Sonia Johnson," 20.

5. Quinn, "A National Force," 398. Quinn believed the Special Affairs Committee purposely kept the First Presidency of the church uninformed of their activities.

6. Johnson, *From Housewife to Heretic*, 330–31.

7. See Sillitoe and Swenson, "The Excommunication of Sonia Johnson," 20.

8. Johnson, Los Altos.

9. Quinn, "A National Force," 390.

10. Karen Timmons Rypka, "Unregistered Mormons Charged with Lobbying against ERA," *Fauquier Democrat*, March 1, 1979.

11. "State Official Probes Mormon Lobbying," *Reston Times*, March 1, 1979. See also "Mormon Group to Register with State," *Reston Times*, March 15, 1979, found in Box 3, Folder 9, SJP.

12. "Contact: The ERA."

13. See, for example, Focus on Salt Lake Sonia Johnson broadcast; and Cheek and Johnson at NOW.

14. Campbell Interview with Swenson.

15. Campbell Interview with Briscoe.

16. Campbell Interview with Swenson.

17. Campbell Interview with Briscoe.

18. Beverly Campbell Interview with Patrick Greenlaw. Item 7, SJAV.

19. Campbell Interview with Greenlaw.

20. Campbell Interview with Greenlaw.

21. Paul Swenson, "Who Is Beverly Campbell and Why Is Everyone Afraid of Her," *Utah Holiday*, February 8, 1980.

22. Campbell Interview with Briscoe.

23. Sonia Johnson on *Midday* in Saint Louis on January 8, 1980, as quoted in Swenson, "Who Is Beverly Campbell," 14.

24. Campbell Interview with Swenson.

25. Campbell Interview with Swenson.

26. Johnson, "Even Institutions."

27. Johnson, Tri-Cities.

28. Johnson, Fresno.

29. Sonia Johnson, Mormons: The Termites in the House of Justice Speech Notes, MS 0287, Box 24, Folder 6, SJP. See also Johnson, Fresno.

30. Johnson, Tri-Cities.

31. Minutes, 16. The full sentence is capitalized and underlined in the original.

32. Minutes, 18.

33. Minutes, 16–18. The phrase "because the prophet has asked me to do it" is capitalized.

34. Campbell Interview with Swenson.

35. Campbell Interview with Swenson.

36. Sillitoe, "Church Politics," 36.

37. Quinn, "A National Force," 384.

38. Johnson, Kalispell.

39. Johnson, "Mormons: The Termites."

40. Johnson Interview with Greenlaw.

41. Sillitoe, "Church Politics," 37.

42. Beverly Campbell on WXYZ Radio, Gerry Pond Audiovisual Files, CHL.

43. "Contact: The ERA."

44. Campbell Interview with Briscoe.

45. Campbell Interview with Briscoe.

46. Linda Cicero, "Mormon Money Worked against Florida's ERA," *Miami Herald*, April 20, 1980.

47. Cicero, "Mormon Money."

48. Cicero, "Mormon Money."

49. Cicero, "Mormon Money."

50. Diane Divoky, "Mormon Muscle . . . Members' Funds Fought ERA," *Sacramento Bee*, April 19, 1980.

51. Cicero, "Mormon Money."

52. Minutes, 2.

53. Johnson, Provo Speech Excerpts.

54. Johnson, Provo Speech Excerpts.

55. Johnson, Los Altos.

56. Johnson, Los Altos.

57. Focus on Salt Lake Sonia Johnson Broadcast.

58. Johnson, Kalispell.

59. Johnson, "Even Institutions."

60. Johnson, Tri-Cities.

61. Minutes, 12.

62. "Contact: The ERA."

63. Johnson on the LDS Church, Hinckley, and the ERA.

64. This narrative is constructed from accounts from Campbell, Hayes, Smith, and Johnson. See KTVX Interview with Beverly Campbell, January 16, 1980, CHL; Campbell on WXYZ Radio (Campbell appears with *Donahue* producer Darlene Hayes); Barbara B. Smith, *A Fruitful Season* (Salt Lake City: Bookcraft, 1988), 163; Interview with Sonia Johnson, KRNG Tulsa, CHL. This is a recording of a radio show called *Nightline* hosted by David Stanford.

65. Johnson, Provo Speech Excerpts.

66. Johnson, Provo Speech Excerpts.

67. Johnson, Provo Speech Excerpts.

68. Johnson, Provo Speech Excerpts.

69. Johnson, Provo Speech Excerpts.

70. See Taylor G. Petrey, *Tabernacles of Clay: Sexuality and Gender in Modern Mormonism* (Chapel Hill: University of North Carolina Press, 2020).

71. Johnson, Provo Speech Excerpts.

72. Take2.

73. Johnson Interview with Greenlaw.

74. Take2.

75. Campbell Interview with Greenlaw; Campbell Interview with Gibson. Gibson's show argued before the broadcast that the *Donahue* episode in which Johnson appeared did not meet the criteria outlined in the "fairness doctrine," a federal law that required anyone who held a broadcast to expose the public to differing viewpoints on controversial public issues.

76. Barbara Smith and Beverly Campbell, *Donahue* Program, December 19, 1980, Item 24, SJAV. Smith seemed to be talking here primarily about women's

organizing in Virginia but may also have been including Johnson's excommunication. The episode was heavily promoted by Heber G. Wolsey, director of public relations for the church, who sent a letter on church letterhead to a number of public communications associates, asking them to notify their local priesthood leaders so they could "publicize and promote" the episode to generate the "widest possible exposure." See Heber C. Wolsey to Public Communications Associate, February 8, 1980, Beverly Campbell Papers, Box 7, Folder 3, CHL.

77. Swenson, "Who Is Beverly Campbell."

78. Campbell on KWMS.

79. Johnson Interview with Greenlaw.

80. Take2.

81. Johnson, Tri-Cities.

82. Johnson, Tri-Cities.

83. Johnson, Kalispell.

84. Johnson, Fresno.

85. Johnson, Tri-Cities.

86. Johnson, Provo Speech Excerpts.

87. Sonia Johnson *Today* Show, January 9, 1981, Gerry Pond Audiovisual Files, CHL.

88. See Petrey, *Tabernacles of Clay*.

89. In discussion with the author, January 22, 2023.

90. See "Hundreds Protest over Prop. 8," *Deseret News*, November 7, 2018, accessed June 10, 2023, https://www.deseret.com/2008/11/7/20284735/hundreds-protest-over-prop-8; "Mormon Church Draws Protest over Marriage Act," *New York Times*, November 8, 2008, accessed June 10, 2023, https://www.nytimes.com/2008/11/09/us/09protest.html; Colin Moynihan, "At Mormon Temple, a Protest over Prop 8," *New York Times*, November 13, 2008, accessed June 10, 2023, https://archive.nytimes.com/cityroom.blogs.nytimes.com/2008/11/13/at-mormon-temple-thousands-protest-prop-8/.

91. Kristen Moulton, "Mormon Women Again Turned Away from Priesthood Meeting," *Salt Lake Tribune*, April 11, 2014, accessed September 6, 2022, https://archive.sltrib.com.

92. Jon Herskovitz, "About 1,500 Mormons Resign from Church in Protest of Same-Sex Policy," Reuters, November 15, 2015, https://www.reuters.com/article/us-utah-mormons-samesex/about-1500-mormons-resign-from-church-in-protest-of-same-sex-policy-idUSKCN0T414G20151115.

93. Courtney Tanner, "Excommunicated Bishop Leads 800 in a March to End Child Abuse and Hold All Religions Accountable," *Salt Lake Tribune*, October 5, 2019, updated October 10, 2019, https://www.sltrib.com.

94. "Nearly 200 People Protest Possible Excommunication of Former LDS Bishop Sam Young," abc4utah, September 9, 2019, accessed July 2, 2022, https://www.youtube.com/watch?v=sGxEoKWb9GI.

95. Joanna Brooks, quoted in Joanna Brooks, Sonia Johnson, and Kate Kelly, "Mormon Feminists and the Equal Rights Amendment," *RadioWest* podcast, June 9, 2022, accessed September 30, 2022, https://radiowest.kuer.org/show/radiowest/2022–06–09/mormon-feminists-and-the-equal-rights-amendment. For a chronology of the excommunication of the September Six, see Lavina Fielding Anderson, "The LDS Intellectual Community and Church Leadership: A Contemporary Chronology," *Dialogue: A Journal of Mormon Thought* 26, no. 1 (Spring 1993): 7–64.

96. See "John Dehlin, Popular Mormon Podcaster, Excommunicated by Church," *NBC News*, February 10, 2015, updated February 10, 2015, https://www.nbcnews.com; and Sarah Pullium Bailey, "Mormon Sex Therapist Has Been Expelled from the LDS Church," *Washington Post*, April 14, 2021, accessed September 6, 2022, https://www.washingtonpost.com/religion/2021/04/22/mormon-sex-therapist-expelled-lds-church/.

97. See Lauren Larson, "The Mormon Church vs. the Internet," *The Verge*, July 1, 2019, accessed September 6, 2022, https://www.theverge.com/2019/7/1/18759587/mormon-church-quitmormon-exmormon-jesus-christ-internet-seo-lds.

98. Robert Lamb, "Housewife Turned Heretic," an undated article from unnamed source found in unprocessed Sonia Johnson collection, Merrill-Cazier Library, Special Collections and Archives Division, Utah State University. Italics in original.

99. Linda Sillitoe, "Off the Record: Telling the Rest of the Truth," *Sunstone*, December 1990, 17.

100. Lindsay Hansen-Park, "Yes, It Is Possible to Both Be Mormon and a Feminist," Quartz Media, accessed March 5, 2018, https://qz.com/768890/yes-it-is-possible-to-both-be-mormon-and-a-feminist/.

Bibliographic Essay

1. Johnson, Kalispell.

2. Johnson, "Patriarchal Panic."

3. Johnson, "Even Institutions." Reprinted in local newspapers sometimes under different title. See, for example, "The Case against Me Is Grievously Distorted," *The Record* (Hackensack, NJ), January 9, 1980, newspapers.com.

4. Mary L. Bradford, "All on Fire: An Interview with Sonia Johnson," *Dialogue: A Journal of Mormon Thought* 14, no. 2 (1981): 44. See also Mary L.

Bradford, "The Odyssey of Sonia Johnson," *Dialogue: A Journal of Mormon Thought* 14, no. 2 (1981): 14–26.

5. Bradford, "All on Fire," 41.

6. Bradford, "All on Fire," 34; emphasis in original.

7. Bradford, "All on Fire," 44.

8. Langlois and Johnson, 9.

9. Langlois and Johnson, 14.

10. Langlois and Johnson, 17.

11. Johnson, *Going Out of Our Minds*, 16.

12. Johnson, "In Defense of Equal Rights." See also Sonia Johnson, "In Defense of Equal Rights," *Women's Press*, November/December 1981, in Herstory Archive: Feminist Newspapers, Archives of Sexuality and Gender, Gale Primary Sources, accessed January 1, 2022, http://tinyurl.galegoup.com/tinyurl/8UPed3.

13. Press coverage of Congressional Union activities appear in Box 4, Folder 6, SJP.

14. Eric Nalder, "Two ERA Supporters Chain Themselves to Mormon Temple," *Seattle Post-Intelligencer*, November 16, 1980, Folder 24, Box 9, SJP.

15. Press coverage of these events are located in Box 9, Folder 24, SJP.

16. Press Release, May 18, 1982, Box 14, Folder 4, SJP. Press coverage of this event can be found in Box 41, Folder 3, SJP.

17. Stephanie Mansfield, "Coming Home after the ERA Fast," n.d., found in Box 41, Folder 3, SJP.

18. Bayles, "Nonfiction in Brief."

19. Johnson, *Housewife*, 393.

20. "Sonia Johnson: The Answer Is Feminism," *Off Our Backs*, October 1984, 20, https://www.jstor.org/stable/25794543.

21. Ed Rogers, "Feminist Opens Presidential Race," *Washington Times*, n.d., CHL.

22. Citizen's Party, Sonia Johnson—Citizen for President, Statement to the Press, October 24, 1983. Found in MS 225, MERA Papers, Box 7, Folder 9, USU.

23. Citizen's Party, Sonia Johnson—Citizen for President.

24. Sonia Johnson, "Want a Real Debate? Invite Me," *USA Today*, October 5, 1984.

25. *Sonia Johnson and Richard Walton v. Federal Communications Commission*, 829 F.2d 157 (1987).

26. Johnson, *Going Out of Our Minds*, 20; Sonia Johnson, "Going Farther Out of Our Minds Part I," filmed [unknown], YouTube video, 58:11, posted [unknown], accessed November 9, 2019, https://www.youtube.com/

watch?v=VGDfCQmKuPA and https://www.youtube.com/watch?v=CyLYZ
5bKXuc.

27. Johnson, *Going Out of Our Minds*, 81.

28. Johnson, *Going Out of Our Minds*, 125–75.

29. Johnson, *Going Out of Our Minds*, 148. See also Citizen's Party, Sonia Johnson—Citizen for President.

30. Johnson, *Going Out of Our Minds*, 145.

31. Johnson, *Going Out of Our Minds*, 247.

32. Johnson, *Going Out of Our Minds*, 248.

33. Johnson, *Going Out of Our Minds*, 263.

34. Johnson, *Going Out of Our Minds*, 349.

35. Johnson, "Going Farther Out of Our Minds."

36. Mary Daly, *Gyn/Ecology: The Metaethics of Radical Feminism* (Boston: Beacon, 1978). Daly discusses the concept of patriarchal reversal most thoroughly in *Beyond God the Father: Toward a Philosophy of Women's Liberation* (Boston: Beacon, 1973).

37. Johnson, *Going Out of Our Minds*, 292.

38. Johnson, *Wildfire*, 52.

39. Johnson, *The Ship*, 90.

40. Johnson, *The Ship*, 282.

41. Sonia Johnson in discussion with the author, September 24, 2022.

42. Sonia Johnson and Jade DeForest, *Out of This World: A Fictionalized True-Life Adventure* (Estancia, NM: Wildfire Books, 1993), 354.

43. Johnson, *SisterWitch Conspiracy*, xii.

44. See Bryan Sykes, *Adam's Curse: A Future without Men* (New York: Norton, 2004); Bryan Sykes, "The Future of Sex: The Death of the Y Chromosome," *Mental Floss*, March–April 2008.

45. Johnson, *SisterWitch Conspiracy*, 28.

46. Johnson, *SisterWitch Conspiracy*, 218.

Index

Note: Throughout this index, "SJ" refers to Sonia Johnson.

Adix, Shauna M., 45, 63–64
African Americans: Black freedom movement in the U.S., 7; Black male LDS priesthood and, 52, 53
American Psychological Association (APA), SJ speeches (1978, 1979), 38–39, 40, 55, 63, 86
Arizona: LDS anti-ERA campaign in, 30–31; SJ moves to, 21
Associated Press, 11, 39, 53, 56

Barrett, Michael, 34, 35
Bayh, Birch, 11
Beers, Robert, 29, 60, 75
"Bellevue 21" protests (1980), 17, 89
bloggernacle, 82, 83
Bradford, Mary L., 87–88
Bradley, Martha Sonntag, 54
Briscoe, David, 53, 56, 59
Brokaw, Tom, 80
Brooks, Joanna, 82
Bushman, Claudia, 7
busing, 28, 71–72, 75

Cahill, Jerry P., 41, 44, 73–74
California: fundraising for Florida state senate campaigns, 72, 73–74; LDS anti-ERA campaign in, 30–31, 44; Proposition 8 protests, 81; SJ campaign for U.S. President and, 19, 90–91; SJ first teaching job in Palo Alto, 4–5, 11

callings/priesthood callings (LDS): impact of female removal from, 44; nature and importance of, 69–70; for women's citizen council participants, 70–71
Campbell, Beverly: as cochair of the Virginia LDS Citizens Coalition (VACC), 29, 53, 54, 58, 67–71, 74–78; LDS public relations for resisting the ERA and, 56–60, 62–63, 67–69, 72–74, 77–79; SJ *Donahue* appearance and, 76–78; women "fronting" for men and, 76–79
Cannon, Elaine Q., 53
Cannon, George Q., 54, 55
career of SJ: education and, 1, 4–5, 6; first teaching job in Palo Alto, CA, 4–5, 11; motherhood and, 4–5, 6, 9, 19–20
Casa Feminista, 21
church and state: distinctions between, 40, 57, 60–61; early LDS lack of distinction between, 48; separation of, importance of, 57–60
The Church and the Proposed Equal Rights Amendment (Gray Book), 25–26, 27, 54, 58, 60
church discipline. *See* excommunication (generally); excommunication of SJ
Church News, 25
Church of Jesus Christ of Latter-day Saints (LDS): book on early Mormon women's history, 7; church prophets, 23, 48, 49, 51, 54, 57; early support for women's rights, 7–8, 11; Equal Rights Amendment and (*see* Equal Rights Amendment [ERA]);

Church of Jesus Christ of Latter-day Saints (LDS) (*continued*): excommunication of SJ (*see* excommunication of SJ); First Presidency (*see* First Presidency [LDS]); headquarters in Salt Lake City, 8, 13, 28–33, 35–37, 41, 42, 52, 65–66, 68, 69, 74, 81, 86, 87; insider vs. outsider perceptions of language, 60; LDS feminists in Utah and, 7–8, 32, 38, 44, 45, 87; missionary program, 14, 37–38, 61–62, 86; political power of, 31–32, 33, 41–42, 45, 57–58, 72, 73–74; Primary organization, 5; public relations office, 37, 41, 52, 56–60, 73, 77; Quorum of the Twelve, 26, 68; Relief Society (*see* Relief Society); semiannual General Conferences, 13, 53, 81; SJ baptized as member, 3; Special Affairs Committee (*see* Special Affairs Committee [SAC]); temple recommends, 44; women's organizations (*see* citizens councils/women's citizen councils); Young Men organization, 5; Young Women organization, 4, 5, 53
citizens councils/women's citizen councils, 66–80; activism under authority of the Special Affairs Committee (SAC), 12, 28, 66–67, 68, 71, 76, 87; busing women to activities, 28, 71–72, 75; as extensions of church patriarchy (SJ), 66–67; LDS fundraising methods and, 72–74, 86; LDS men organizing women and, 65–74; as lobbying groups of women, 28, 67, 75–76; Missouri Citizens Council, 66, 69, 71; in Nevada, 66; priesthood "callings" for participants in, 44, 69–71; as private citizens vs. church representatives, 71–75, 87; in Virginia (*see* Virginia LDS Citizens Coalition [VACC]); women "fronting" for men and, 66, 74–80
Citizen's Party, 19
Clyde, Craig, 59
Common Cause magazine, 88–89
Consumer Party (Pennsylvania), 19
Contact (television series), 59
cosmology, 95–96

Daly, Mary, 93
DeForest, Jade, 20–21; *Out of This World*, 95
Dehlin, John, 82
Democratic National Convention (1980), 16
Deseret News, 25

Dialogue: A Journal of Mormon Thought, 5, 7, 87–88
Donahue (television program), 14, 43–44, 76–78
Donahue, Phil, 76–78

England, Eugene, 5
The Ensign magazine, 25–26, 53, 54
Equal Rights Amendment (ERA): *The Church and the Proposed Equal Rights Amendment*, 25–26, 27, 54, 58, 60; civil disobedience and demonstrations, 10–12, 17–18, 21, 88–90, 91; defeat (1982), 12, 15, 18, 86, 89; introduction to U.S. Congress (1972), 25; LDS feminist support for, 7–8, 9–13, 16–18, 29–32, 43–46, 49; LDS fundraising for anti-ERA campaigns, 72–74, 86; LDS opposition to, 1–2, 7–16, 23–32, 33, 37–42, 44, 46, 47–60, 62–63, 65–74, 77–79, 86; LDS position as secular political stance, not religious stance, 47–48, 56–64; LDS publications opposing, 25–27, 53, 54; misleading claims concerning, 58–59; Mormons for ERA (MERA) and, 10–12, 13, 29–32, 44, 69; NOW and, 7, 8, 13, 17–18, 37–38, 45, 61–62, 86; press/media coverage of LDS resistance to, 13, 22–23, 30–33, 37–38, 39, 41, 47, 49–50; SJ conversion to (1977), 1–2, 9–10; SJ speech at Democratic National Convention (1980), 16; SJ testimony before U.S. Senate Judiciary Committee (1978), 11, 12, 13, 16, 32, 85–86; state ratification votes and, 7, 10, 13, 18, 25, 37–38, 42; StopERA organization, 24, 29; text of, 9, 45; threats to supporters of, 44–45; Washington, D.C., demonstration for passage of (1978), 10–11
The Equal Rights Dilemma, 26
Evans, Bill, 66
excommunication (generally): bishop Sam Young challenge to sexually explicit interviews with LDS youth, 81, 82; membership withdrawal instead of, 15, 82; as most severe LDS disciplinary action, 14; of other LDS feminists, 21, 43–44, 81–83; same-sex marriage as LDS excommunicable offense, 81
excommunication of SJ, 32–46; appeals of LDS decision by SJ, 15, 41–42; archive/information sources on, 2–3, 36–37;

excommunication letter, 36–42, 63; false doctrine argument and, 4, 9, 14, 34, 36–43, 44; formal and informal charges, 36–43, 61–62; injustices to SJ, 34, 35, 40–43, 46, 47, 62; LDS rejection of Equal Rights Amendment and, 1–2, 10–12, 13, 14, 23–32, 35–37; nature and impact of excommunication, 1, 14–16, 22–23, 45–46; as prelude/blueprint for LDS discipline against other feminists, 81–83; press/media coverage and responses to, 2, 13, 14–15, 22–23, 24, 33–38, 41–44, 47, 52, 53, 56–57, 62, 69, 76–78, 80; pretrial and trial meetings in Virginia Bishop's Court, 14, 33–37, 62; SJ critique of LDS leadership and, 14, 15, 16, 35–36, 40, 48, 49, 63–64; SJ divorce from husband and, 1, 15, 16; SJ feminism following, 1, 16–21, 42–46, 56, 81–83; SJ private meeting with the Special Affairs Committee (SAC), 15, 76; SJ request for extension of time, 34, 42
Exponent II (newsletter), 7–8, 85–86

false doctrine argument, of SJ, 4, 9, 14, 34, 36–43, 44
feminine theology, 82–83
feminism (generally): Equal Rights Amendment and (see Equal Rights Amendment [ERA]); feminist awakenings, 7–10; LDS feminists in Utah, 7–8, 32, 38, 44, 45, 87; LDS feminists in Virginia, 8–12, 13, 28–29, 32; movement toward female equality with men, 23–24; "new left" and, 7; United Nations declaration of International Women's Year, 8; working definition of, 88
feminism of SJ, 3–21; adolescent challenges to LDS attitudes toward sexuality, 4; archive/information sources on, 2–3, 36–37; career and (see career of SJ); civil disobedience/demonstrations and, 10–12, 17–18, 21, 88–90, 91; confrontational style of, 16–17; critiques of LDS in, 2, 4–5, 8–18, 23–24, 35–36, 40, 48, 49, 63–74; early feminist stirrings, 3–6; Equal Rights Amendment and (see Equal Rights Amendment [ERA]); feminist awakenings of, 8–10; Korea and, 6; lesbian relationships and, 16, 18, 20–21, 94–96; Mormons for ERA (MERA) and, 10–12, 13, 29–32, 44, 69; motherhood and (see motherhood, of SJ);

national women's movement and, 8; Palo Alto liberals and, 4–5, 11; post-excommunication, 1, 16–21, 42–46, 56, 81–83 (see also excommunication of SJ); public feminism of, 10–21; reading in feminist theory, 8–9; "savage misogyny" accusation, 15, 36, 38, 62–63, 87; second-wave feminist movement and, 7; sexual double standard and, 4, 16; Wildfire feminist community in New Mexico and, 20, 95; "woman gatherings"/"woman culture" to counteract patriarchy, 19
Feminist Studies, 88
First Presidency (LDS), 66, 68, 70, 71; anti-ERA campaign of, 9, 12, 25–27, 31, 52–53; Black male LDS priesthood and, 52, 53; call to political activism of LDS congregations, 12, 53, 70, 71; Spencer W. Kimball (as president), 12, 15, 30, 39, 42, 45, 49, 50, 52, 54, 57, 75; LDS correlation wave (1960s) and, 5; official statements opposing the ERA, 9, 25–28
Flake, Kathleen, 45, 48
Florida: California fundraising for state senate campaigns in, 72, 73–74; LDS anti-ERA campaign in, 30–31
Fluhman, J. Spencer, 48, 60
Foster, Rodney P., 66
Frame, Kelli, 45
Freund, Paul A., 58
From Housewife to Heretic: husband, Rick, and, 4; LDS position on the ERA and, 10–11, 13–14; nature of memoirs and, 2–3; on the *New York Times* bestseller list, 14, 90; reprints in 1983 and 1989, 90; sexual double standard and, 16
fundraising, 71–74; for anti-ERA campaigns, 13, 72–74, 86; in California, for Florida state senate campaigns, 72, 73–74; citizens councils/women's citizen councils (LDS) and, 72–74, 86

gender/gender roles: International Women's Year (IWY), 8; in Korea, 6; lesbian relationships and, 16, 18, 20–21, 81, 94–96; same-sex marriage, 81; SJ confrontation of LDS double standard and, 4, 16; SJ U.S. presidential campaign (1984) as patriarchal, 19, 90–91. See also feminism (generally); feminism of SJ; Mormon patriarchy/patriarchal priesthood

120

Georgia: LDS anti-ERA campaign in, 30–31; LDS fundraising methods in, 72; SJ moves to, 21
Gibbons, Francis M., 42
Gibbs, Charlie, 15
Gibson, Roy, 78
Glaser, Vera, 43–44
Going Out of Our Minds (1987), 18–19, 91–92
Goldsmith, Judy, 18
Gray, Frederick T., 67
Gray Book (*The Church and the Proposed Equal Rights Amendment*), 25–26, 27, 54, 58, 60
Greenlaw, Patrick, 24, 78

Harris, Alvin (father): Mormonism of, 4; SJ attitudes toward, 3
Harris, Ida Lavina Howell (mother): birth of SJ, 3; excommunication of SJ and, 35; Mormonism of, 4; SJ attitudes toward, 3–4
Hatch, Orrin, 11, 32
Hayes, Darlene, 76–77
Helfer, Natasha, 82
Henry, Patrick, 89
Hinckley, Gordon B., 12, 15, 28, 31, 66, 68, 71, 76
Horwitz, Susan, 18, 20
The Hungry Heart (Nicholson), 21

Illinois: defeat of ERA (1982) and, 12, 15, 18, 86, 89; LDS anti-ERA campaign in, 30–31; LDS fundraising methods in, 72; Women's Fast for Justice, 18, 21, 89–90
International Women's Year (IWY): declaration by the United Nations (1975), 8; state conventions in the U.S., 8

Jesus Christ: excommunication of SJ and, 34; SJ's adolescent challenges to LDS attitudes toward sexuality and, 4; SJ's mother's approach to teachings of, 3–4
Johnson, Eric (son): birth, 4; SJ as "nonmother" and, 20–21; SJ love of, 5
Johnson, Kari (daughter): birth, 4; SJ as "nonmother" and, 20–21; SJ love of, 5
Johnson, Marc (son): birth, 4; SJ as "nonmother" and, 20–21; SJ love of, 5–6
Johnson, Noel (son): birth, 6; SJ as "nonmother" and, 20–21
Johnson, Richard (Rick) T. (husband): divorce from SJ, 1, 15, 16; education and career of, 4, 6, 8; international travels and residences of, 6, 8; marries SJ, 4; move to Virginia, 6, 8; relationship with SJ, 6; removes membership records from LDS in solidarity with SJ, 15
Johnson, Sonia Ann Harris (SJ): accusations of "savage misogyny," 15, 36, 38, 62–63, 87; baptism as member of LDS (1944), 3; birth (1936), 3; Casa Feminista, 21; critiques of LDS and leaders, 2, 4–5, 8–18, 23–24, 35–36, 40, 48, 49, 63–64; current status of, 21; dangers of alliance of religion and politics, 53, 57–58, 60–61, 67, 73–74; divorce from husband, 1, 15, 16; early years and family background, 3–4; education and career of, 1, 4–6, 8, 11; ERA and (*see* Equal Rights Amendment [ERA]); excommunication from LDS (*see* excommunication of SJ); feminism of (*see* feminism of SJ); health concerns, 18, 20; international travels and residences of, 6, 8; kinship with LDS women, 78–80; LDS fundraising methods and, 72–74, 86; LDS men organizing women and, 65–74; legacy of pain of confronting the LDS church, 83; lesbianism and, 16, 18, 20–21, 94–96; marries Rick Johnson, 4; as Mormon housewife, 1, 5–6, 7–9, 12; motherhood and (*see* motherhood, of SJ); moves to Arizona, 21; moves to Virginia, 6, 8; move to Georgia, 21; mystical approach to Mormonism and, 3–4, 6, 8–9, 80–81; public speaking (*see* public speaking, by SJ); teaching position in Palo Alto, 4–5, 11; U.S. presidential campaign (1984), 19, 90–91; Wildfire feminist community in New Mexico, 20, 95; women "fronting" for men and, 66, 74–80; works of (*see* works of SJ)

Kalispell, Montana, speech (1979), of SJ, 37–38, 61–62, 86
Kelly, Kate, 21, 81, 82
Kimball, Spencer W., 12, 15, 30, 39, 42, 45, 49, 50, 52, 54, 57, 68, 75
Knight Ridder Newspapers, 11

LaBrosse, Marty, 89
Ladd, Don: as chair of LDS Washington D.C. area Public Affairs Council, 28; as co-organizer of VACC, 12, 28–30, 66, 70–71; as Regional Representative, 12, 28–30, 66
Langlois, Karen, 88

Latta, Marilee, 44

Latter-day Saints (LDS). *See* Church of Jesus Christ of Latter-day Saints

Lee, Rex E., 58

Lefevre, Don, 37, 41, 52, 56–57, 59

Leone, Mark, 43

lesbianism, of SJ, 16, 94–96; Chris and, 20; Jade DeForest and, 20–21, 95; Susan Horwitz and, 18, 20; *The Ship that Sailed into the Living Room* (1991) and, 94–95

LGBTQ population: California Proposition 8 protests, 81; U.S. Supreme Court ruling on same-sex marriage, 81. *See also* lesbianism, of SJ

Lindsay, Richard, 28, 52–53

Lowe, Julian: as co-organizer of VACC, 12, 28–30, 66, 68, 70–71; as Regional Representative, 12, 28–30, 66, 68, 70–71, 74–76

MacKay, Kathryn, 66

marriage: centrality of heterosexual marriage and family to LDS theology, 26–28, 55; divorce of SJ from husband, 1, 15, 16; same-sex marriage as LDS excommunicable offense, 81. *See also* Relief Society (LDS)

Maxwell, Neal A., 15, 76

McDannell, Colleen, 44

membership withdrawal, 15, 82. *See also* excommunication (generally)

Miami Herald, 73–74

missionary program (LDS), 14, 37–38, 61–62, 86

Missouri: International Women's Year conference in, 8; LDS anti-ERA campaign in, 30–31, 70; Missouri Citizens Council (LDS), 66, 69, 71

Montana: Kalispell speech (1979) of SJ, 37–38, 61–62, 86; LDS anti-ERA campaign in, 30–31, 37; NOW campaign for ERA in, 37–38, 61–62, 86

Mormon patriarchy/patriarchal priesthood: Black male priesthood and, 52, 53; brainwashing of women to hate themselves, 93; excommunication of SJ and (*see* excommunication of SJ); female disengagement from, 93–94; female internalization of, 16–19, 80–81; LDS correlation wave (1960s) and, 5, 12; as LDS founding principle, 22–24, 27, 50–51; LDS fundraising methods for anti-ERA campaigns, 72–74, 86; LDS male religious authority over women and, 5, 22–23, 31,

50–51, 57–58, 65–74; LDS opposition to the Equal Rights Amendment and, 1–2, 7–16, 23–32, 33, 37–42, 44, 46, 47–60, 62–63, 65–74, 77–79, 86; LDS women "fronting" for men and, 66, 74–80; male alliances to support, 16, 17; male privilege of SJ sons and, 19–20; patriarchal reversal (Daly), 93; patriarchy in genetic nature of men, 96; priesthood "callings," 44, 69–71; revelation and, 27, 47–56; sexuality/sex and, 4, 26–28, 81, 94–95; as a sham (SJ), 8–9, 63; SJ contempt for hierarchy, 20–21; SJ critique of LDS leadership, 2, 4–5, 8–18, 23–24, 35–36, 40, 48, 49, 63–64; SJ rage toward, 10; Special Affairs Committee and (*see* Special Affairs Committee [SAC]); women and men as distinct classes of people, 5, 92–93. *See also* Church of Jesus Christ of Latter-day Saints

Mormons for ERA (MERA), 10–12, 13, 29–32, 44, 69

Mormon Sisters: Women in Early Utah, 7

Mormon Women's Forum, 45

motherhood, of SJ: ambivalence concerning, 5; births of children, 4, 5–6; feminism of SJ and, 4–5, 6, 9, 19–21; as form of entrapment for women, 20–21; Eric Johnson (son) and, 4, 5, 20–21; Kari Johnson (daughter) and, 4, 5, 20–21; Marc Johnson (son) and, 4, 5–6, 20–21; Noel Johnson (son) and, 6, 20–21; Korean experiences with work and, 6; LDS claims of ERA threats to mothers, 26; SJ as Mormon housewife and, 1, 5–6, 7–9, 12; SJ becomes a "nonmother," 20–21; work of women vs. men and, 6

National Organization for Women (NOW): Equal Rights Amendment and, 7, 8, 13, 17–18, 37–38, 45, 48, 61–62, 86; as key feminist lobbying organization in the U.S., 7; Montana campaign for ERA, 37–38, 61–62, 86; SJ failed campaign for presidency of, 18; SJ leads civil disobedience conference, 17–18; SJ opposition to methods used by, 17–18; Utah campaign for ERA, 45

Nevada: citizens councils/women's citizen councils in, 66; LDS anti-ERA campaign in, 12, 30–31, 66; LDS call to political activism and, 12; LDS fundraising methods in, 72

122

New Mexico: Casa Feminista, 21; SJ moves to, 20, 21; Wildfire feminist community, 20, 95
Newsweek magazine, 37–38
New York Times, 14, 90
Nicholson, Zoe, 21

Ordain Women, 81, 82
Out of This World (1993), 95

Packer, Boyd K., 66
Pageant magazine, 9–10
Park, Benjamin E., 48
patriarchy. *See* Mormon patriarchy/patriarchal priesthood
Paul (apostle), 54
Peace and Freedom Party (California), 19
Peterson, Mark E., 4
Petrey, Taylor G., 80
President of the church: Spencer W. Kimball as twelfth President, 12, 15, 30, 39, 42, 45, 49, 50, 52, 54, 57, 68, 75; role of, 47–49; Wilford Woodruff as fourth President, 54. *See also* First Presidency (LDS)
press/media coverage: of excommunication of SJ, 2, 13, 14–15, 22–23, 24, 33–38, 41–44, 47, 52, 53, 56–57, 62, 69, 76–78, 80; of LDS fundraising methods, 73–74; of LDS opposition to the ERA, 13, 22–23, 30–33, 37–38, 39, 41, 47, 49–50; media misquoting by SJ, 12, 28, 74; media misquoting of SJ, 3, 15, 23, 36, 37–38, 62–63, 86, 87; of pro-ERA activism, 13; recent, of SJ, 21; "savage misogyny" accusation, of SJ, 15, 36, 38, 62–63, 87; of SJ testimony before the U.S. Senate (1978), 11, 32
Primary organization (LDS), 5
prophet, follow the, 27, 54–56
public speaking, by SJ, 19–20, 37, 86; American Psychological Association conferences , 38–39, 40, 55, 63, 86; at the Democratic National Convention (1980), 16; "Going Farther Out of Our Minds" (1987), 92; Kalispell, MT, speech (1979), 37–38, 61–62, 86; LDS anti-ERA campaign and, 33; NOW presidency campaign (1982), 18; for NOW pro-ERA campaign, 13, 18, 86; "Off Our Pedestals, or the Chronicles of the Uppity Sisters" (1979), 38, 87; U.S. presidential campaign (1984), 19, 90–91; U.S. Senate Judiciary Committee testimony (1978), 11, 12, 13, 16, 32, 85–86. *See also* works of SJ

Quinn, D. Michael, 27–28, 45, 54, 66

Rampton, Sheldon, 33
Reagan, Ronald, 45
Relief Society: correlation process in stripping autonomy of, 12; excommunication of SJ and, 76–77; as LDS adult women's organization, 5, 27–28, 86; LDS anti-ERA campaign and, 25, 52, 66, 71–72, 86; as private citizens vs. church representatives, 71–72; *The Relief Society Magazine,* 5
Republican National Convention, 17
revelation, 47–56; church opposition to the ERA and, 27, 31–32, 40, 47–48, 49–56, 59, 61; origins and nature of, 48; "patriarchy is a sham" (SJ) and, 8–9, 63
Rigby, Hazel, 8, 9, 10–11
Rigby, Ron, 8
Roueche, Earl, 15, 34, 41, 42
Rutgers College, 4

Sacramento Bee, 73
same-sex marriage, 81
"savage misogyny" accusation, of SJ, 15, 36, 38, 62–63, 87
Sawyer, Diane, 22
Schlafly, Phyllis, 24, 29, 58
second-wave feminism. *See* Equal Rights Amendment (ERA); feminism (generally); feminism of SJ; National Organization for Women (NOW)
sexuality: bishop Sam Young challenge to sexually explicit interviews with LDS youth, 81, 82; centrality of heterosexual marriage and family to LDS theology, 26–28; lesbianism of SJ, 16, 18, 20–21, 94–95; rape and violence against women as institutions of patriarchy, 92; same-sex marriage, 81; SJ as "nonmother" and, 20–21; SJ confrontation of LDS double standard and, 4, 16; SJ on sex as patriarchal act, 20. *See also* LGBTQ population
Shipps, Jan, 7–8
The Ship that Sailed into the Living Room (1991), 94–95
Sillitoe, Linda, 22, 24, 33, 66, 71, 72, 82
The Sister Witch Conspiracy (2010), 80–81, 95–96
SJ. *See* Johnson, Sonia Ann Harris (SJ)
Slechta, Joyce, 44
Smith, Barbara, 25, 27, 52, 76–77
Smith, Joseph, 23, 48, 54

Index

Snyder, Tom, 14, 15
South Carolina, LDS anti-ERA campaign in, 30–31
Special Affairs Committee (SAC): Gordon B. Hinckley as head of, 12, 15, 28, 31, 66, 68, 71, 76; nature of, 52–53, 65–66; as overseer of the citizens councils, 12, 28, 66–67, 68, 71, 76, 87; SJ post-excommunication private meeting with members of, 15, 76
speeches, of SJ. *See* public speaking, by SJ
Stafford, Belle, 25
StopERA organization, 24, 29
Swenson, Paul, 59, 68, 70, 79

Tanner, N. Eldon, 54, 55
Temples: "Bellevue 21" protests, 17, 89; LDS headquarters in Salt Lake City, 8, 13, 28–33, 35–37, 41, 42, 52, 65–66, 68, 69, 74, 81, 86, 87; recommends and, 44; SJ demonstrations at, 17, 81, 89
Thielke, Linda, 38
Today show, 80
Tomorrow show, 14, 15
Twelve/Quorum of the Twelve (LDS), 26, 68
Tyler, Jan, 8, 15

Ulrich, Laurel Thatcher, 7
United Nations, International Women's Year (1975), 8
United Press International (UPI), 11, 38
U.S. presidential campaign (1984), of SJ, 19, 90–91
U.S. Senate Judiciary Committee, testimony of SJ (1978), 11, 12, 13, 16, 32, 85–86
USA Today, 91
Utah: confrontational tactics of LDS feminists in, 32; ERA ratification vote, 25; International Women's Year convention (1975), 8; LDS feminists in, 7–8, 32, 38, 44, 45, 87; LDS headquarters in Salt Lake City, 8, 13, 28–33, 35–37, 41, 42, 52, 65–66, 68, 69, 74, 81, 86, 87; media coverage of SJ excommunication in, 13; *Mormon Sisters: Women in Early Utah*, 7; NOW campaign for ERA in, 45; Utah Equal Rights Coalition, 44; Utah Women's Conference (1979), 38, 87
Utah Holiday magazine, 59
Utah State University, 4

Virginia: confrontational tactics of LDS feminists in, 32; excommunication of SJ in (*see* excommunication of SJ); LDS anti-ERA campaign in, 9, 30–31 (*see also* Virginia LDS Citizens Coalition [VACC]); LDS feminists in, 8–12, 13, 28–29, 32; Earl Roueche as LDS Stake President, 15, 34, 41, 42; SJ and family moves to, 6, 8
Virginia LDS Citizens Coalition (VACC): activism under authority of the Special Affairs Committee (SAC), 12, 28, 66–67, 68, 71–75, 76, 79; co-organizers of, 12, 28–30, 66, 68, 70–71, 74–76; as lobbyist with the state of Virginia, 67, 75–76; men organizing the women and, 65–74; organizing meeting, 12, 28–29, 30, 54, 60, 70–71, 74, 75–76; original cochairs, 29, 53, 54, 58, 67–71, 74–78; priesthood "callings" for participants in, 44, 70–71; Regional Representative Lowe and, 12, 28–30, 66, 68, 70–71, 74–76; women "fronting" for men and, 67–73, 74–79

Walton, Richard, 91
Washington, D.C.: confrontational tactics of LDS feminists in, 32; demonstration for passage of ERA (1978), 10–11; LDS Washington D.C. area Public Affairs Council, 28; media coverage of SJ excommunication, 13
Washington Herald, 43–44
Washington Post, 30, 47, 57, 62, 87
Washington Star, 43
Washington state: "Bellevue 21" protests, 17, 89; LDS anti-ERA campaign in, 30–31
Weathers, Diane, 37–38
White, O. Kendall, 54
Why Mormon Women Oppose the ERA, 26
Wildfire (1989), 19–20, 93–94, 95
Wildfire Books, 90
Wildfire feminist community (New Mexico), 20, 95
Willis, Jeffrey, 14, 32–42, 61–62, 87–88
Withers, Maida, 10–11
Wolsey, Heber G., 77
"woman gatherings"/"woman culture," to counteract patriarchy, 19
Woman's Exponent (newsletter), 7, 8, 85–86
women's citizen councils. *See* citizens councils/women's citizen councils
Women's Fast for Justice (Illinois), 18, 21, 89–90
Women's Fireside, 53
Wood, Arlene, 77

Wood, Teddie, 10–11
Woodruff, Wilford, 54
works of SJ, 85–96; "Even Institutions Reap What They Sow," 87; *Going Out of Our Minds*, 18–19, 91–92; "In Defense of Immoderation," 88–89; *Out of This World*, 95; published interviews, 87–88; *The Ship that Sailed into the Living Room*, 94–95; *The Sister Witch Conspiracy*, 80–81, 95–96; "Telling the Truth," 92; "Want a Real Debate? Invite Me," 91; *Wildfire*, 19–20, 93–94, 95. See also *From House-wife to Heretic*; public speaking, by SJ

Young, Brigham, 48
Young, Neil J., 54–55
Young, Sam, 81, 82
Young Men organization (LDS), 5
Young Women organization (LDS), 4, 5, 53

Zundel, Jean: as cochair of the Virginia LDS Citizens Coalition (VACC), 29, 67
Zussman, John Unger, 45, 63–64